IN THE COMFORT
OF HIS ARMS

Scripture quotations from

IN THE COMFORT
OF HIS ARMS

Carolyn Bradley

with guest authors

To order additional copies of this book, contact:
Xlibris
1-888-795-4274
www.Xlibris.com
Orders@Xlibris.com
550289

CONTENTS

PART ONE

PART TWO

PART THREE

PART FOUR

PART FIVE

"The eternal God is your refuge, and underneath are the everlasting arms."

(Deuteronomy 33:27)

To all children everywhere, with much love:

May you always dream and hope and love, and may we adults give you a peaceful and loving world in which to live and grow.

Acknowledgments

With thankfulness and deep appreciation for their beautiful contributions to this book:

Jeff Bradley
Megan Boniti
Rachel Boniti
Laura Boniti
Mary Evkovich
Bernadette Finley
Karen Majoris-Garrison
Sarah Walker-Haymond
Barbara Hervey
Rev. Dr. Christina Hosler
Claude Kinty
Edward J. Kochman Jr.
Ashley Krnaich
Michael Majoris
Trinity Majoris
Kristen Malinowski
Colleen Mindzak
Kathy Nagy
Josie Pate
Noreen Saxon
Carrie Oliver-Schultz
Lynda Cross Slowikowski
Susan Spencer-Smith
Sharon Ann Steele

Susan E. Wagner
Marilynn Walker
J. Michael Walker
Margie Zellars

Preface

In the Comfort of His Arms is a book of trust, hope, love, and wonder. We first trust God for all our needs. We then receive hope, love, and wonder as we realize the truth of His grace, beauty, and help in all.

We are all God's children. He holds us, loves us, and cares for us in a unique and masterful way.

Trusting God enables His full power to encircle us with help and hope, for He is faithful to His promises.

"Come to Me, all You who are weary and heavy laden, and I will give you rest. Take My yoke upon you, and learn from Me, for I am gentle and lowly in heart, and you will find rest for your souls" (Matthew 11:28–29).

As *we* come to God, *He comes* to us, with His refreshment, peace, and love.

In the Comfort of His Arms is a grace-filled book, for *God is mighty, God saves*, and *God meets all our needs*.

We rest . . .

. . . *in the comfort of His arms!*

PART ONE

"The eternal God

is your refuge

and underneath are

the everlasting

arms"

(Deuteronomy 33:27)

Not One!

The foolish men who cry and say,
"There is no God—so why should we pray,
To a Being not there, a myth, a lie,
We'll do our thing—before we die."

We have no rules—we can do all,
And sin becomes our daily call—
And the despots too, show mercy to none—
But *who* can make a *tree*? *Not_one*!

With all the works of man on earth,
We cannot give him a second birth,
To be so great, so grand you see,
That he *indeed* could make a *tree*!

And the God of all the Universe looks down,
And cries His tears for every town—
Which chooses to stray from His law and grace—
For they do not *want* to see His face.

Oh world of woe—Oh world of sin—
We have only let the darkness in—
The light is there—but we refuse to see,
And call it a myth—unreality.

We choose to stay in the darkness dim,
And do not set our souls toward Him,
Oh foolish world—how often you don't see,
The darkness is really the unreality.

May all on earth abide His call
To heed His mercy, love, and all,
And rest within His arms of grace,
And long to see His loving face!

Oh God of all the Universe be,
Kind and holy to such as we,
For we ask for guidance, strength, and love,
To serve you, *our God in Heaven above.*

Oh foolish men, how often you say.
"I will not serve, I will not pray,"
But no matter what all men have done,
They cannot make a tree—
        Not one!

A Message

When I was a little girl, I loved when the snowflakes would start to fall from the grey leaden sky and, later, when the sun would come out, the touch of diamonds was everywhere. We would watch the snow mounting, piles and drifts and little slopes, and we would know that it was time to play—and play we did! What a winter wonderland for children—playing in the snow, making snowmen, finding pieces of coal for two bright eyes, a woolen scarf, a carrot for his nose, and three more shiny coal buttons going down his chest.

Snowball "fights" and sled-riding down the slope in the alley adjacent to our backyard were other "treasures" as well as making a snow "igloo" with the snow piled high above our heads. We had unimaginable fun— and the days were glorious and wonderful, bright with the prospects of the day's happenings.

One thing I did alone, though, was something I had started doing as a young child, and that was to write a message to God in the snow. I would use my gloved finger to write in the soft powdery snow—a prayer—so that He could see. I would write the words "I LOVE YOU, GOD" in very large letters and then step back to admire my handiwork. It was beautiful, I would think, and then I would look up to the sky, and *say* the words I had written—"I love you, God." I wanted Him to see what I had written. I knew He was so far up in heaven, but I knew He looked down on earth, surveying it with His watchful eyes. I wanted Him to see my words—written in the snow.

As I grew, that was still a part of my time—being out in the snow— and I would write my message of love to Him.

As a young mother, when I was outside in the snow with my three children, I would take time for my special message to God.

I kept this up as the years went on, and now, as a grandmother, and with the grandchildren growing up strong and true and beautiful as my children did, I'd give thanks to my Heavenly Father for all His amazing and powerful gifts to me—of home and family and love beyond measure.

The other day, the snow fell again, and as I trudged through our yard, looking at all the beauty and majesty all around me, my gloved hand went again to the newly fallen snow, and I wrote, in large letters, stretching across the yard,

"I LOVE YOU, GOD"

I hope He saw it!

We *all* have a song in our hearts, and we need to sing that song, for even if we feel alone, someone may hear it and then sing their song too and make *our* hearts *rejoice*!

The Calling Bird
Jeff Bradley

One bird perched alone, on dark pine-needled branch.
The snow fell then, tumbling down, it fell upon him.
It touched his feathers. Like soft, electric shocks,
barely apparent, they landed.
The snow fell all about, surrounding,
and yet, his voice was silent.
The sounds of flakes spoke softly—
One by one, he heard them, riding the air around.
A rustle, and continue . . .
To rest at last, lie soft—on blanket white, below.
"Tick," he heard, attending—and so there contemplated . . .
But still remained unspoken, ever pondering.
The dark, almost black-green evergreen,
peppered white, the candied frosting, everywhere.
All around, he watched this.
And then, he wished to sing . . .
But he was all alone—and so there remained,

and kept the song within.
The snow knew, and wished to ask,
what might he have to say.
It would have rejoiced to hear, for to become
what song withheld could be.
But the bird did bide, and held inside—
the song within his heart.
A forsaken call for none to hear,
it died upon this branch.
A beautiful branch, both dark and bright.
Of shattered whisper, dark and light.
One bird alone, not knowing the loss,
or yet, what was to come,
Lifted his head, discerning the sky
And the snow . . . fell everywhere.

Holy Water

Karen Majoris-Garrison

It hadn't rained for months. The parched, faded ground reminded me of myself. I walked along our fence, noticing the wilted flowers I had planted in the spring. Because of the drought, they had never thrived.

"Everything is dying, Lord," I whispered aloud.

Within two years, my husband and I had lost several friends, then my mother-in-law, and, soon after, my father-in-law. Although it had been nine months since my father-in-law's death, my heart ached. He'd been a vital part of our family. "It was only supposed to be routine surgery," I reminded the Lord, recalling the medical staff's errors. "And now he's gone."

I neared our porch, spotting the empty doghouse that awaited our dog's return. Even our beloved pet had been taken from us. One month after my father-in-law's failed surgery, Meshach, our black Labrador, disappeared. *Where were you, Lord?* my heart cried. *Why didn't you keep those we love from harm? We trusted You!*

The previous year had sapped my strength, and like the earth beneath me, I felt withered. Even the Bible, which I routinely depended on to overcome obstacles, lay unopened on my nightstand for months.

"Give me something, Father," I pleaded. "Anything to understand why You'd allow tragedies to those who have faith in You."

And He did.

I remembered Job 13:15: *Though he slay me. I will trust Him.*

Shaking my head, I wondered about the Lord's sense of humor. *Though he slay me, I will trust Him?* Was that verse supposed to make me feel better?

After heading into my house, I retrieved my Bible. My heart raced as I studied Job. Astounded at his declaration of trust after so much suffering, I read, reread, and deliberated over the entire book. During that time, something happened inside of me. My spirit absorbed the power of God's word, and I felt my spiritual drought ending.

The book of Job never did answer my question of "why" but reminded me of "who" God is. No matter what, no matter what trials or tragedies, I must trust Him. In His ways and not mine. I thought of my previous prayers concerning my loved ones. I had trusted that the Lord would answer my requests *my* way, not that I'd trust Him in His ways.

It had become night by the time I finished reading. I slipped outside to gaze at the stars and contemplate all that I'd read. As I lifted my head toward heaven, I felt raindrops.

Smiling, I lifted my hands in worship. My tears flowed, mixing with the rain's steady rhythm. Soaked, I stood there, absorbing what the Lord so freely gave.

And like the water, the holy water that descended from above to replenish the barren earth, God's word replenished my soul. They were one and the same. Quenching, cleansing, and renewing.

Stepping back inside the house, I grinned—knowing that tomorrow my flowers would be standing tall—just like I would be.

In Loving Memory of
Timothy S. Bradley

Tim passed away at the age of fifty-two from cancer. He touched us all in a very special way. Tim's way was to smile through it all. He endured his illness with all the human emotions that we have, but with a great difference. There was an acceptance there, a serenity deep down that he wouldn't fight against life but accept it as it came.

His smile was there for us all—and he leaves behind these smiles which are like beautiful jewels for us all.

Tim sent us a card to "thank us for our prayers." He appreciated everyone praying for him. And he wrote, "The prayers have made me strong."

But *Tim* made *us all* strong, to see him go through his illness with such grace, dignity, perseverance, trust, hope, love, and strength. He is an example to us all, showing us the beauty of life and the quiet acceptance of what life brings to us all. He taught us to do the best that we can, to pray to God for our needs, and to accept what happens in the end.

Tim accepted everything, and he is a beautiful example of *hope* for us all!

The Basket

Lynda Cross Slowikowski

Through the eyes of my memory
I can still see
The basket.
In it are buttons to be sewn back on
And bright spools of thread.
Lots of needles,
Different sizes
For patching and repairing.
The hoops are readied
To be used to embroider
Flowers and leaves
And other designs.
Proudly she turned
Plain table covers,
Pillowcases and sheets
Into something amazingly beautiful
And to be treasured through the years.
But her family
She sewed together
With the threads of her love.
It was her art
And we are forever blessed by it.

Hope
Carrie Oliver-Shultz

Carrie and her husband lost their firstborn daughter, Anna Danielle, at 23 weeks and 2 days into the pregnancy due to preterm labor on July 2, 2013.

This is a letter she wrote the following year.

JANUARY 2, 2014

Although I have plenty to be thankful for this past year, I have to admit that I am so relieved to know that 2013 has come to an end. I know it's just a number, but we as humans mark our years with significance as to what happens in our lives.

So often we hear questions like "What year did she pass away?" or "What year did you graduate?"

We label events in our lives with years. It's just how it is. We even refer to our age by the number of years we have been alive. Not months, days, or hours. And it's not that I believe that certain years are "bad" or "good." Every year . . . every day . . . that we're alive is good. Because God is good.

But this past year of 2013 had its challenges for my husband and me and our family. It had its moments of joy, happiness, and laughter. But it was difficult not to allow the pain, sadness, and grief to overshadow them.

Still, we chose joy.

And this year, we choose hope.

I'm not foolish to think that this coming year won't have its share of challenges and heartaches. That is a part of life, and it is in those "stretching" times that we grow. In fact, my relationship with the Lord grew more intense than it has ever been through the grief and pain of this past year. When you get to a point where all you have is God, you can either lean on Him or turn away. And I knew in my heart that turning away would only cause me more pain and heartache. I need Him with every fiber of my being, and I found that to be true more this year than I ever have in the past.

One of my favorite scriptures came into my life a few years ago, when our church was focusing on the life of St. Paul for a whole year. This scripture was chosen as the "theme" for the year as we studied his life and his writings. It's taken from Paul's letter to the Romans:

Therefore, since we have been justified through faith, we have peace with God through our Lord Jesus Christ, through whom we have gained access by faith into this grace in which we stand; and we rejoice in our sufferings, because we know that suffering produces perseverance, perseverance character, and character hope; and hope does not disappoint us, because

God has poured out his love into our hearts by the Holy Spirit, whom he has given us. (Romans 5:1–5)

St. Paul demonstrated hope in his writings and actions. He inspires me to do the same. I refuse to live in fear after all that has happened in this past year. I just received a beautiful message from a very spiritual friend of mine over Facebook today:

It is indeed possible to start again, to find joy, even after it seemed lost forever . . . through the Grace of God! I've prayed, and Jesus has heard my plea. I stand on His Word, and I truly believe that whatever I ask in His name, I will receive. Thank you Jesus! Have faith and believe . . . never doubting my friend.

How true those words are.

Two months after we lost (our daughter) Anna in July, we unexpectedly lost my husband's father to a sudden heart attack. We were spinning in grief, pain, and confusion. I then began experiencing odd heart palpations and bizarre thoughts going through my mind. Suddenly, for the first time in a very long time, I was afraid of death. And I would lie awake at night, afraid to fall asleep, fearing that I was not going to wake up the next morning. It was like this bondage of fear had taken a hold of me and wouldn't let go.

Given the history of heart disease in my family, I did pay a visit to my cardiologist to make sure that there was not a physical problem going on. After a thorough examination, he found nothing to be alarmed about. He believed that it was stress that was causing anxiety.

I then met with a very good therapist that I have been to in the past to talk with her about what was happening. I left her office amazed after she shared with me how powerful the mind can be and how it can affect our bodies in ways that we can't control. Just having the knowledge of how that can happen left such a huge impact on me. From that day on, my new mantra was "Everything is okay." The more I told myself that, the more I believed it.

I never had another heart issue again after that. The negative and fear-filled thoughts in my mind were replaced with positive and life-giving ones.

One week later, I discovered I was pregnant again.

I'm absolutely in awe of how the Lord works. I cried out to Him for help, and He answered me.

Again, I refuse to live in fear. I refuse to live in darkness. I crave the light . . . the true light.

As I stood over my daughter's grave on Christmas Eve just over a week ago, I wept with sadness over the pain of how much I wished she was here with her daddy and me and her family. But as I sobbed, my hands slowly moved to my belly. Under my heavy winter coat and the mounds of warm clothes that I was wearing on that cold, snowy day . . . and beneath my very skin . . . life was growing there again.

Hope. It does not disappoint.

The Yellow Bird

Karen Majoris-Garrison

Hope sometimes visits us in different shapes and sizes. On an autumn day in October, it came to a young couple from our church in the form of a yellow bird.

Scott and Janice had tried for many years to have a baby, and when their son, Scotty, entered the world, the church celebrated right along with them. Soon, however, the doctors diagnosed Scotty with serious heart problems.

Rallying behind the young family, our church supported and reminded them of God's promise to never fail or forsake his children. Nine months passed, and Scotty's doctors had determined that he needed open heart surgery. His chances of surviving the operation were slim, but without it, his chances of living past his first birthday were slimmer.

Throughout his ordeal, one thing had become amazingly clear about Scotty. He absolutely loved the color yellow. Whenever he'd catch a glimpse of the bright hue anywhere, he'd squeal in delight. Even his nurses had added a touch of yellow to their uniforms when caring for him.

Sadly, Scotty's operation hadn't been a success, and the attempt to save his little heart failed.

His parents, grief-stricken, had escaped to a friend's vacation home soon after the funeral. Weeks passed, but the gaping wound left by Scotty's absence remained unbearable. Until one sunset evening as Scotty's parents walked along the beach. Once a threesome, they now clutched each other's hands with the dark realization that Scotty's tiny fingers would never again be clasped between theirs. With too heavy a cross to bear, they felt alone in their grief until a reminder of hope expelled the darkness.

It appeared in the form of a bright yellow bird that had landed between them as they walked along the water's edge. Neither parent had ever seen such a bird before, nor, unbelievably, had it scurried or flown away, but it continued to scamper between them on their barefooted journey in the sand.

Soon, the bird's comforting presence filled them with peace. The peace granted to believers in 1 Thessalonians 4:13–14: *"But I would not have you be ignorant, brethren, concerning those that have fallen asleep, lest you sorrow as those that have no hope. For if we believe that Jesus died and rose again, even so God will bring with Him those who sleep in Jesus."*

After they'd made it back to their beachfront house, the bird remained, studying them for a few moments before lifting its wings and heading upward toward the sky.

While watching its graceful flight, they had imagined Scotty, in the presence of God, soaring high above the clouds and making his way to that incredible yellow ball for a warm kiss upon his chubby cheek.

Today, Scott and Janice's tragic cross to bear is lighter by the trust that carries it. When questions of "why" plague them, they can be reminded of God's faithfulness to walk beside them and His willingness to lift them when they fall.

After all, hope had come to them. It appeared in the form of a yellow bird—a gentle messenger fashioned by the Creator's own hands, and carrying with it seeds of comfort, promise, and *sunshiny* love.

A Pilgrim's Journey

Rev. Dr. Christina Hosler

Josie P.

Over the years, I have had an opportunity to study Celtic spirituality. Celtic Christians believe that we are all on a journey, together, from birth to death. Our paths go in different directions, but along the way our road intersects with the path of others. At times we meet a person at that intersection who becomes a lifelong friend, others are acquaintances for a time, and there are others with whom we never really interact. Each of these persons, known or unknown, are fellow pilgrims on life's journey.

The idea of being a pilgrim on a journey became very real to me a few months ago as I was blessed to have the opportunity to spend a few weeks on pilgrimage in Ireland and Scotland. A pilgrimage is not the same as a vacation in that a pilgrimage is intended to be transformational; it is an inner journey as well as an outer journey. As

I was first introduced to my travel companions for the next ten days, I did not immediately make the connection that we were pilgrims. At the moment, they were strangers whom I had never seen before and knew nothing about.

As our pilgrimage began, each of our individual paths intersected with the others as we broke bread together, prayed and worshiped together, climbed mountains together, and had fellowship together. Whether well-known or little-known, we were no longer unknown; we were no longer strangers. We were fellow pilgrims on the journey of life whose lives intersected at a certain time and place for a certain purpose, and as a result, we were all changed forever. As I sat on a rock on the Isle of Iona, I meditated and pondered this realization: people are only strangers because we haven't taken a moment to know and be known.

Being of Scotch-Irish heritage, I wondered about my ancestors who may have been in that very place. While I didn't know them personally, I felt an amazing sense of belonging, of connectedness to the early people of that land. They were pilgrims on a journey, and our paths intersected in that place as I thought about the life they lived, the battles they fought, and the faith they held on to. I was grateful to be in that place at that time, and I was grateful for all those pilgrims who had gone before me. As I prayed and meditated, the Spirit convicted me that every person is significant; every person has been uniquely and intentionally created. Psalm 139:13–14 came to mind, which reminds us: "For you created my inmost being; you knit me together in my mother's womb. I praise you because I am fearfully and wonderfully made; your works are wonderful, I know that full well" (NIV).

This conviction of the Spirit was confirmed as we went to evening prayer in the Iona Abbey, where we shared communion with people from all over the world. We were invited to tear off a piece of bread from the common loaf and hand it to the person next to us indicating "the Body of Christ." We then drank from the common cup and offered it to our neighbor, "the Blood of Christ." The woman from whom I received the Sacrament did not speak English, and yet there was an understanding. We were united as sisters in Christ regardless of our language. Several hundred people from all over the world, speaking different languages, sharing the Lord's supper together, united through our Lord Jesus Christ. There was not a stranger in the abbey that evening. As God's creations, we are all pilgrims on the journey of life.

Having a grasp of this *concept*, I wondered how my interactions with other people might be different if I began to *apply* the concept to my life. I wondered what might happen if I treated every single person as a fellow sojourner. I wondered how I might be more Christ-like as I considered no one a stranger. When I returned home, I began to live this out. I became more intentional about viewing people as fellow pilgrims, and I noticed a change in me. For example, the long checkout line at the grocery store was an opportunity to have a conversation with the person in front of or behind me. Instead of being frustrated at the long line, I realized that every person in that line has a story; every person has a desire to be known. My simple "Hi! How are you today?" makes them no longer invisible; suddenly, they are known by another.

I applied this concept on the road. This may be helpful to those of you who deal with occasional bouts of road rage, or at least road irritation! Merge points on the highway are a great illustration of our journey intersecting with other pilgrims. If we consider those on the road fellow pilgrims instead of idiots who don't know how to use a turn signal, or goofballs who try to cut you off, it makes a big difference in the journey for both you and the goofballs—I mean pilgrims—on the road. The folks on the road have a place to get to just like me, so I try to make their journey a little easier for them.

As I daily apply the concept of pilgrimage, I find that there are less strangers in my life. I've learned to appreciate the uniqueness of individuals, and I am truly interested in where they are on their journeys. I challenge you to experiment in your own life. You are a pilgrim on this journey of life. Every person with whom you cross paths is a fellow sojourner. At every intersection, God may be trying to use you to be a blessing to another pilgrim, so don't let the opportunity pass you by. May your journey be filled with exciting twists and turns, and may God bless your every step.

Seeking

Claude Kinty

As I walk the road of life seeking God's face and wisdom, each revelation has taught me that I have so much more to learn.

Isaiah 55:8–9 says, "For My thoughts are not your thoughts, neither are your ways, My ways saith the Lord, for as the heavens are higher than the earth, so are My ways higher than your ways, and my thoughts than your thoughts."

Friendship: A Triple Blessing

Susan Spencer-Smith

"I do not call you servants any longer, because the servant does not know what the master is doing; but I have called you friends, because I have made known to you everything that I have heard from my Father."   *~Jesus in John 15:15*

Christian friendship holds great power.

I realized today, after a bit of Bible study, that Christian friendship is not just a gift of the Holy Spirit.

Christian friendship is a triple whammy, for it is a gift of God through Jesus Christ *and* a gift of the Holy Spirit *and* a gift of the believer. I'll try to explain.

We begin with love as God's idea: "For God so loved the world that he gave his only Son, so that everyone who believes in him may not perish but may have eternal life" (John 3:16).

Of course, Jesus lived out God's love—in his teachings, his miracles, his signs, his humble obedience even unto death.

Before his sacrifice on the cross, Jesus commanded us to love as he did: "This is my commandment, that you love one another as I have loved you" (John 15:12).

What Jesus commands, the Holy Spirit enables. Guided by the Holy Spirit, Paul encourages Christian love in 1 Corinthians 13, beginning, "If I speak in the tongues of mortals and of angels, but do not have love, I am a noisy gong or a clanging cymbal."

This kind of love—love that is patient, kind, humble, courteous, joyful, honest, enduring, trusting, hopeful—is unquestionably a fruit of the Holy Spirit.

Now come back to John 15, where we see that Jesus also says, "You did not choose me but I chose you."

Jesus reminds us that friendship is a gift of the giver, not something seized by the receiver.

The source of selfless love is God through Jesus Christ. The power to love as Jesus loves is a gift of the Holy Spirit. But the choice to love as Jesus loves is a choice of the giver.

Your Christian friendship, therefore, represents a triple blessing, or a triple anointing, because

- *Jesus Christ* models God's perfect love (the first blessing).
- *The Holy Spirit* enables the love of Christian friendship (the second blessing).
- *You* choose to be a Christian friend (the third blessing).

Beloved, your Christian friendship holds extra power because of *your part* in it.

The Holy Spirit's gifts are given to build God's kingdom.

Every time you offer Christian friendship, you are building God's kingdom!

Adoration

Father, I pray for you to be loved
   as You deserve to be loved,
   and praised as You deserve to be
      praised,
   and blessed as You deserve to be
      honored and adored—
throughout all ages. Amen!

Knowing

   Father, I love You. I know You know what
I am going through. You know the pain,
   the heartache, the distress.
   Take this from me, kind Father, but if I
   must endure longer, give me strength,
      forbearance and help to continue on.
   I love You, Father.
         You are my *rest*.
         You are my *hope*.
         You are my *peace*. Amen

Ellie Marie

We heard your tiny heart beating . . . Our hearts were pulling for you
. . . Come on, little girl . . . keep beating . . . Keep living . . . put up a
good fight.

Only twenty-two weeks and coming too soon,

But your little heart kept a steady rhythm—and it was the most
beautiful sound on earth.

We were allowed to be with your mother and father in the delivery
room.

We waited, we prayed—we hoped.

C'mon, little girl, c'mon.

But then, right toward the end . . . it stopped . . . and angels came for you, to take you on your flight to heaven.

Did you see your family crying leaden tears? Your body was stillborn then, and we each held you so lovingly in our arms, wrapped in a tiny white blanket. White was appropriate for an angel—a new saint—a holy child of God. Your soul was totally white.

The waters of baptism were poured over your still small frame.

"I baptize you, Ellie Marie, in the name of the Father and of the Son and of the Holy Spirit."

A child of God sent on her way, clothed in garments of light—in the very sanctity and grace of God.

We hope you took a backward glance to see your family grieving there—

For we will be with you in heaven, for all eternity.

See you then, Ellie Marie,

    See you then.

In loving memory of

Ellie Marie Llewellyn
My great-granddaughter

Ocean Sunrise

Michael Majoris

Just before first light, the world is magnificent, calm, and perfect. The anticipation consumes me. I see a ray of a faint orange, glowing and streaming through the horizon, and my heart flutters. The beauty is overwhelming, and I cannot look away.

I spend the next few minutes pondering what is more brilliant—the way the colors shine through the ever-changing cloud formation, or the process itself. It is as if I am watching a painting evolve in slow motion with each frame its own masterpiece. Every day, a different, grand portrait is produced.

I want to stay in this moment for a long while. All my thoughts, fears, and anxieties and anything I hold in my heart—good, bad, or unresolved—are temporarily washed away like the tide reaching the shore. The sand, for the time being, becomes clean, level, and uniform with no trace of prior footsteps. I look ahead and start running, uninhibited.

I am not alone. Others are visible, but I cannot hear any dialogue. They are transfixed, and I observe my morning companions as they watch the first part of the singular circle shape take its form. Are they here to find comfort, pray, or have some reflection time? Does the emerging sunlight provide a spark of drive and inspiration for a very early workout? Or is it simply sharing joy in the company of a spouse or loved one that they seek? Whatever the reason, the collective silence speaks volumes.

What if the soothing ocean waves is God's way of hushing and creating a profound stillness? Is the rise and fall of the tide His constant reminder of life's possibilities and obligations, which we must learn to tread in harmony? Yes, many come to the shoreline at dawn, with hope present for all.

An hour or so has passed, and I must walk back through the beach, with all its peaks and valleys and twists and turns in the sand. Getting a good footing takes some effort, but mostly it is just a feel.

As the sky turns brighter, I feel the shadows creep back, and I think how I can obtain a little bliss each day without the spectacular views and relaxing sounds. Should I shake the dust off the good book and read in some scenic outdoor spot? How can I best find the ocean sunrise in my own daily routine?

I return again to my place of morning solitude with my family as we decide to take one last beach walk at the end of our splendid four-day adventure. My son and I move hand in hand as we navigate together ahead of my wife and daughter. I know he can sense my sadness. He then pauses and, as exuberant as a darting dolphin, tells me not to worry, that this is just the beginning. It is a simple statement, but for me, it is as vast and rich as the endless waters. The ocean sunrise has been and will always be there—in the light of my loved ones' eyes and in the radiance of their smiles, accompanied by waves of laughter and words of encouragement. In this, I envision the first rays of a new morning and the wide-open flat sand, and my heart runs free.

He Does Hear All Our Prayers!

Margie Zellars

"Do not be anxious about anything, but in every situation, by prayer and petition, with thanksgiving, present your requests to God. And the peace of God, which transcends all understanding, will guard your hearts and your minds in Christ Jesus" (Philippians 4:6–7 NIV).

Have you ever felt like no one is listening to you, not even God when you are praying to Him? I feel that way at times. Sometimes, I feel that I am invisible as I speak to people, and they seem not to hear me or even care what I say. It can be so frustrating.

There is one occasion that particularly comes to my mind. It was a time of great sadness and trial for me and my husband. He was diagnosed with pancreatic cancer. On one particular Thursday, as I sat by his bedside at the hospice center and watched him slip away, I began to wonder if God really did hear and answer my prayers. You see, my husband was absolutely positive that he was going to get a miracle, and he would be healed. Ron even called others he had heard had pancreatic cancer and encouraged them to have faith and believe in God and His healing power. My husband was a man of deep faith and loved Jesus Christ with all his heart and being. His battle with this terrible disease was inspiring and difficult to watch as he suffered with the pain and agony of pancreatic cancer.

People all over the world were praying for him. His faith never wavered during this time at all. But for me, on that particular Thursday when I sat there watching him sleep and look so frail and failing, I could not help but wonder if God did hear my prayers at all. Ron was in and out of the hospital so very much over those past four months. When he was in the hospital, I stayed day and night most of the time when they allowed me to do so. He would sleep a lot from the pain medication that they gave him, so I would sit and read the Bible and inspirational books of hope and pray for hours on end. That is what we are told to do by Paul: do not be anxious for anything but by prayer and petition with thanksgiving; give it to God, and he will grant the peace that surpasses all understanding in your times of need especially. I must admit at that point I could not feel that at all. All I saw was my husband getting weaker and slipping away quickly over the course of this week.

As he was lying there resting comfortably, I read my Bible and said several prayers. Even though I was not sure if I should say a novena, a very special lady sent me the Prayer of St. Therese to say for Ron. My grandmother's name was Therese, and she was such a woman of faith that the very name of Therese touched my heart. As these were desperate times, I felt I should say this prayer and had been doing so daily for several weeks. When I finished praying the prayer of St. Therese, I began to weep and sob. My heart ached as I looked over at my sweet husband so sick and so hurting. I felt so much anger inside and asked God if He was listening to my prayers. I asked Him if He was listening to anyone's prayers as so many people were praying for my husband, and all I saw was that his condition was worsening and he was not getting the healing or the miracle he was so sure that God would grant him. At that moment, I felt abandoned by God and very much broken and hurt as the man that God had brought into my life as my husband was being taken away from me. The pain and sorrow was so deep and intense, and the feeling of extreme loneliness was almost more that I could bear. Just when I asked Him if He was listening to me, a nurse walked into the room with a dozen of red roses from an organization that sends roses to hospice care patients and their families every Thursday. The nurse set them on the table and walked out. I began to cry, but this time, it was tears of joy. God sent me a message that yes, indeed, He heard all our prayers and mine in particular, and He was answering them. How did I know this? St. Therese is known as "The Little Flower" as she loved flowers. Many of the pictures of her show her holding flowers, mostly roses. The picture on the novena was of her holding the cross and a red rose. Coincidence? I think not, as there are no coincidences in life. God is always there showing us that He is with us always. We are told in Jeremiah 29:11–13, "For I know the plans I have for you," declares the Lord, "plans to prosper you and not to harm you, plans to give you hope and a future. Then you will call on me and come and pray to me, and I will listen to you. You will seek me and find me when you seek me with all your heart." We just do not always see Him at work in our lives at that moment. Sometimes, we need to look back on a situation to see Him with us. But at that moment, I had no doubt He heard my prayers. From that day until my husband went home to heaven on Sunday afternoon, God granted me the peace that surpasses all understanding that I never understood what it meant until He granted it to me at that moment in time to help me get through the most difficult journey of my life, walking the final days with my husband and his battle with cancer.

You see, the moment that Jesus took Ron away from this earthly life, when he took his last breath here on earth, God showed me that Ron took his first breath in heaven. And with that first breath, he got the miracle he prayed for and believed in. He received his heavenly body completely healed with no more pain, no more tears, and no more disease. He was standing in front of Jesus completely healed and covered in the light and peace of his Lord and Savior Jesus Christ. Knowing this gave me that gift of peace that only God can give, the peace that surpasses all understanding. And what a gift that is!

Sometimes we all feel that God is not listening when life gets difficult and our trials seem so overwhelming. This is when we need to get down on our knees and give all situations to God with prayer and petition and with thanksgiving and present your requests to Him. God hears and answers all prayers always. It may not be the answer we want or think we should get, but He does answer all prayers. He is just waiting for us to come to Him and give all our burdens over to Him and let Him care for us. Remember, He loves you always, especially when you do not love yourself. It is not always easy to understand why things happen the way they do and why people suffer with disease, brokenness, and so many tragedies in life. What I want to encourage you to do is to continue praying to and trusting in Him. I hope that my experience will show you that God is listening to you even when you feel He is not. May you feel His presence surrounding you always and allow Him to be your best friend even when you feel all alone and feel like no one cares. Know this: Jesus cares for you, and He is always a prayer away. God does hear our every prayer!

Losing a beloved dog—
the memories and . . .

A Tribute . . . to Logan

(our beautiful chocolate Labrador)
Jeff Bradley

The first day I loved you . . . six little chocolate drops.
She pointed—"This one is special, not like the other ones.
Your eyes said, "Pick *me*, trust me . . . I'll love you till I die.
Logan, I didn't know you were telling the truth.
How fast ten years went by . . .
Now, I'm lost in this wilderness of loss.
No matter how much I cry, no matter how much I try,
I can't bring you back . . .
But the woods are filled with love.
Everywhere, anger and bitterness turn into love.
You gave so much, asked so little,
Loved such simple things,
A walk in the woods, a splash in your pool,
A roll on your back in the snow . . .
The first day you saw me, I hope I returned the same.
These two will love me . . .
Will hold me when it rains . . .

Each day—a gift—sometimes lost by lesser things.
Now time has taken—our love of simple things.
The days to turn weeks into months,
All to memories in the end.
Now I'm lost in this wilderness of loss.
But no matter how much I cry—no matter how I try.
I can't bring you back . . . but the woods are filled with love.
Everywhere, anger and bitterness turn into love.

"The last day you loved me,
You held me when I died.
I knew then, you had loved me—through all the pain and joy.
Someday soon, you'll see *me*, your little
Chocolate Drop.
You'll realize, although time is lost,
Your love, it still remains . . .
We'll walk once more—together again—
Along the road to home . . ."

It's a God Thing

Noreen Saxon

Josie P.

Have you ever had an occasion when something happens and you know the only explanation is that it was divine intervention?

I was an everyday average wife and mother of three children going to church on Sunday and returning to church each Sunday, as I was taught to do as a child and as a young adult. Religion was the foundation of my upbringing.

As a young adult, I would watch my mother hold Bible studies each Monday evening in our home. My mother would also pray along with the rosary that was being said on a television station every afternoon.

I often would feel uncomfortable when I would hear the ladies at the Bible study praying out loud and sharing their stories about God. I would leave the room when my mother prayed the rosary every day also.

I was not anywhere near knowing Jesus as my mother did. Although in the back of my mind I knew going to church was important, I did just that: went to church every Sunday. No more and no less.

What I didn't know was there is more than just going to church!

In brief, I went through a very rough time emotionally in 2005 and several years leading up to that. It was a buildup of several years of confusion, both in my spiritual life and my life that I lived each day. I stopped going to church for a year or so, and I noticed my mind was beginning to spiral out of control, and I didn't know why. I guess the guilt of *not* going to church was getting to me. I decided to return to church each Sunday. Again, I was merely attending Mass as I had been taught.

Then, in the midst of a depressive phase, I sought God, but I was angry because He did not hear my cries for help. I would beg Him to help me. Through divine intervention one Saturday morning, I decided to go to the church; I had no idea *why* I was going to a church at 11:00 a.m. when there was no Mass. I got there and just cried and pleaded for help from God in the dark empty church.

Lo and behold, when I got to my car after I had left the church, I was immediately guided by divine intervention to *return* to the church. I was quite unsure why I was reentering the church. When I did, through many tears, I saw a candle burning in the corner of the church, which indicated that a priest was in a confessional. I entered the room reluctantly and did not know the priest nor did he know me. One of the questions that he asked me was "Ma'am, what exactly is it that you are wanting?"

My quick reply was "I don't want anything materialistic. I just *want to know Jesus the way my mother did.*"

What? Where in the world did that answer come from? I really don't recall ever thinking of that before.

To no avail, I "crashed" and ended up in a hospital needing professional help. When I did go to the hospital, I can truly say that a book was brought to me through divine intervention. I read a few pages of *Power of Living* by Jamie Buckingham, and he recommended putting the book down and asking Jesus to come into my heart but to not expect lightning-fast results.

"What do I have to lose?" I asked myself. At the end of the book, it suggested that the next book I read is the Bible. What? I had a Bible, but I never even *thought* about reading it. It was just something I knew everyone was supposed to have in their home.

From that day forward, I began to see dramatic changes in myself. My outlook on life, people, the church, and my family changed for the better. Joining church groups, praying the rosary, and joining a rosary group and then through divine intervention, I started a Bible study! Does any of this sound familiar?

You got it! I have come to know Jesus the *way* my mother did just as I answered the priest's question in 2005. And I did it all without realizing where I was headed!

God has a plan for all of us as we are told. It sometimes just takes extreme difficulty at times to realize it and accept what He has planned for us. I can say that every trial has been a learning experience and a gift from Him.

So on the days when I cried out for help from God and I was discouraged because I didn't think He was helping me, I have now come to know that He *was there all along*, I was *just not recognizing Him*.

May we all embrace our difficult times knowing that God has a reward ahead for our continued faith in Him!

A Pink Rose

Kristen Malinowski

After receiving the Sacrament of Confirmation at our church, I developed and strengthened relationships that had not been before. Having been a new high school graduate and having had a year of college completed while still in high school, I was preparing to transition from working toward an associate degree to a bachelor's degree. This transition was not as stressful as I had expected. Perhaps it was because I was exposed to college expectations earlier than most because of my relationships with God, family, and friends or maybe because I was dealing with a personal issue.

Upon consulting with various specialists and enduring varying procedures, I had received news that my lifelong dream of bearing my own children was deemed "medically impossible." Seeing my friends pursue relationships and also having children brought this fact home to me even more clearly. Another lifelong dream and passion—to become a teacher—was unintentionally placed on the back burner. I was focused on my grief and jealousy—I did not understand why I was forced to experience this while there are some uncaring people who were able to experience this miracle.

While many aspects of my life were in disarray, I knew I needed to trust God. I constantly recalled prominent events of my life, such as Teens Encounter Christ (TEC) retreats, my Confirmation, relationships with loved ones, and the expectation of a new family member, whom I would soon have the honor of being her *godmother*. My twin brother, who was in his senior year of high school, and I also attended daily Mass.

One particular morning, I was very stressed, this time due to a West Virginia history exam. I had plans of dropping my brother off at school at the regular time of 7:30 a.m., rather than going to Mass, so I could study for my exam at 8:30 a.m. I happened to wake up early and decided at the last minute to go to Mass at 7 a.m. As Mass in our school chapel ended, my brother's Confirmation sponsor and close family friend, who was also a teacher at the school, was talking with our priest. She noted upon walking into the chapel that it smelled like roses. This day also happened to be a feast day for the Blessed Mother. I should note that my Confirmation patron saint is the Blessed Mother Mary, and both mine and my brother's sponsors' names are Mary, and our goddaughter's name is derived from the Blessed Mother.

Before my exam, I decided to run through a local fast-food drive-through to get a breakfast sandwich. Notoriously, orders get messed up there, as did mine that morning. I decided to go in to correct the mishap. While I was standing in line and on my cell phone, I noticed an elderly man staring at me. I smiled and looked back down at my phone. Feeling as if I was being watched, I looked up, and his eyes were still set on me. He had the most beautiful blue eyes and was inviting. I walked over to him thinking he had said something to me. "Excuse me?" I kindly asked. Without ever having said a word to me, this man pulled a pink rose from behind his back. In amazement, I said, "Aw, thank you, but I thought you had to tell me something." His smile eased my worries, and he had still never uttered a word.

I was then called to the counter. I immediately turned around, and this man was gone.

I spoke of this story to others, and all agreed that an angel had visited me. Although I do experience doubts, I trust in God that my dreams will be according to His Will. God has proven that all will be well, through people, events, and His words in Holy Scripture.

I have come to realize that He will not give me what I can't handle. I'm glad that He has such faith in me!

The Hat with the Light

My dad had a hat,
A hat with a light,
He wore it to work,
Amid the day's bright.

He needed the light
For his work that day,
Down in the underground,
So far away.

A miner he was,
Going down deep and true,
Picking out coal,
Not seeing *the blue—*

*of the sky—*for many an hour,
       And then—
Having to do the same thing,
          Again.

It was for many years
That he dug the coal
With a metal pick,
Deep in his soul.

And stooping all day,
Because the shaft was tight,
And needing his hat—
The hat with the light,

To see through,
The dark and the dim,
And this is one of the reasons,
I loved and admired him.

Each day I'd run to meet him,
And I could hardly wait,
To see him coming home each day,
And to meet him at the gate.

I'd see his face blackened,
But his eyes were shining bright,
Below the hat he wore on his head,
The hat with the light.

I reached up to hold his hand,
And *my eyes* were shining bright,
Holding on to the hand of my *dad*,
My dad, with the hat with the light.

I saw his eyes smiling
Under the light,
And I knew that everything
Was going to be all right.

And the hat stood out
About my dad, you see,
As a symbol of all the love
He had for me.

For he had in his heart
A rich legacy,
To make things right,
No matter how they would be.

O Dad, you are in heaven now,
I can picture your smiling face,
Looking down upon us,
Waiting for the grace.

When we will all be together again,
Your little family true,
And we will all share heaven's joys,
Together in heaven with you.

I think one of your trophies there,
Something so dear and bright
Would be on your mantelpiece,
"The Hat with the Light."

For up in heaven's sweet treasures,
I am sure they keep such things,
For they are a part of the journey,
Such as angels getting their wings.

They shine like beautiful trophies
Of jobs and work well done,
And I'm sure that your hat with the light,
Is among the many favored ones.

And I know you'll run to meet me,
And that you will hardly wait,
When you see me coming home,
To meet me at the gate!

A Gathering of Angels

Susan E. Wagner

As a skeptic, I keep my feet firmly rooted in reality, and it was hard for me to believe in what I could not see, touch, prove, or explain. In my heart, I really wanted to believe in miracles, angels, etc., but I was your proverbial "doubting Thomas." But then . . .

It came on insidiously—an intense pressure in my lower abdomen, but no pain yet. Thanks to a pacemaker, I'd almost forgotten I had congestive heart failure (CHF). This was different—very different.

But then the pain started, especially when I ate very much. My appendix had been removed a long time ago, so it couldn't possibly be that. Cutting back on eating a little though did at least make the pain go away. Small in stature and barely weighing 107 pounds, though, it didn't take long before my clothes were getting quite loose. I had lost over five pounds! It was time to see my doctor.

His examination didn't reveal anything, but he prescribed a lotion to massage into my abdomen; it was probably just a strained muscle. Two weeks later, the bottle empty, my symptoms weren't any better. The pressure and pain were increasing. I kept eating less though, which seemed to keep it at a level I could tolerate. In just a few days, my weight went under 100 pounds!

Back to my doctor, and explaining all my symptoms again, he referred me to a specialist. Tests and x-rays were ordered, but nothing significant was found. He prescribed pills anyway because he thought it had to have something to do with my stomach since I wasn't eating much.

At first the pills did bring some relief. Then the dehydration started. I was told to drink lots of fluids, and they went down gladly because I really was very thirsty. I was quite hungry too and trying to eat, but in just a few days, my abdomen became terribly bloated. The intensity of the pressure and pain was becoming intolerable.

Not knowing what else I could do, I continued to eat less, but it didn't have much effect on the pressure and pain, and I knew I must be losing more weight. At the emergency room ER, my weight registered on their scales at only 91 pounds! Admitted to the hospital, I saw more doctors and specialists than I could remember and had more tests and X-rays than I could count. More pills, different pills, were prescribed all with their side effects to which I was vulnerable.

Continuing to complain seemed of no avail. I knew they were trying to help me, but it wasn't long before I could almost read the looks on their faces. I couldn't believe what they were telling me. It was in very carefully chosen words, of course. If I wouldn't take my medications and try to eat more, there wasn't much of anything else they knew to do for me. I couldn't believe them. Hadn't they heard anything I'd been telling them from day one?

Feeling abandoned and like an injured animal that crawls away to hide and lick its wounds, I quit my job, stayed at home, and tried to rest. I couldn't get their last words of advice out of my mind, though. Desperate to escape my symptoms, I became determined to somehow stand the pressure and pain. I took my medications, tried to eat more, and hoped I would heal. It didn't happen.

In just a few days, my legs, feet, and ankles began to swell. I wasn't thinking straight either, but I could remember that the CHF—congestive heart failure—had never done that; it had only affected my lungs.

With the pressure and pain so intense, I was in agony. I couldn't eat or drink anything. Weak, barely able to stand, I got on my scales—my weight had plunged to a measly 86 pounds! All I could see in my full-length mirror staring back at me was a scrawny skeleton, its clothes hanging awry from it. I was starving to death, and I was scared!

That night, all rational thinking gone, my mind began slipping into a dark side of me I didn't know existed. A shred of sanity left, and seeing my Bible on my nightstand, I grabbed it. Frantically leafing through the pages, something seemed different about it. I'm not myself, I thought, and I'm probably disoriented.

Finally, I turned the last page, which should have been blank, except it wasn't. Something was written there, something I had not expected to find: "The Lord works in mysterious ways, His wonders to perform"—in my mother's handwriting. It had been a favorite saying of hers. But how did it get in my Bible? Tears came quickly as I realized what I'd done. Mother had passed years ago, but I'd always kept her old Bible lying beside mine. I'd picked it up instead.

My emotions finally subsiding, suddenly, a strange visage of someone—a man—entered my thoughts. But who was he? All at once, my mind cleared, and I could see him, but his appearance startled me just as it had the first time. It had been a chance encounter.

It happened years ago when I'd gone to the hospital in misery with symptoms of CHF. But when a man of inexplicable countenance walked into my room, I didn't know what to think. He was extremely tall, had a very dark beard, and was even wearing a turban. Seeing my surprised look, he quickly explained that my doctor was out of town, and he was the doctor on call. He'd reviewed my medical records and said I needed a pacemaker implant. I had the implant, and it was such a success that I was even able to continue working. My doctor returned, and I never saw the "strange" doctor again.

Believing the "strange" doctor was my only chance left gave me renewed hope to get through that dark night. The next morning, after much searching, unbelievably, I located him and miraculously secured an appointment.

His examination over, the sound of concern in his voice said it all. "It's your liver! It's engorged! Even with a pacemaker, your heart isn't strong enough to handle that much fluid overload! But what had caused it?" he asked. Thinking back to a few weeks before my abdominal symptoms started, I remembered a severe reaction I'd had to an antibiotic I'd taken for an infection. He thought that highly improbable, but with all my allergies and negative reactions to so many medications, though, it wasn't entirely impossible. That antibiotic just might have been the missing factor that had so stealthily eluded all those other doctors.

"You're going to need several medications that can only be administered in the hospital," he said. "Some will flush out your liver, and others will strengthen your heart to help with that," he added. Placing my trust in him once again, twenty-four hours later, I was eating again! The pressure and pain were almost gone! Several more treatments and I was home again!

Mother's words had been a beacon in that dark night. Clearing my mind, they'd led me back to sanity, to the "strange doctor," and my healing. Do I believe in angels? You bet I do—*heavenly ones* and *earthly ones too*!

Crumbling

Sharon Ann Steele

When we crumble
When we fall
Slumped in stature
Broken and raw
He waits for us
To just look up
With master hands
He works His plan
Remolds the clay
Softened by tears
He puts us together
That we may be better
For Him.

From Him and through Him, and to Him are
all things. To Him be glory—Amen.

There is no grief on earth
like losing a child . . .

A Mother's Grief—Cry of the Wild

Sharon Ann Steele

O woman of such wailing,
Where does that sound come from?
Animalistic cry,
Howl of the wild.

Groaning forces erupt,
Within blocked walls spew forth,
Broken dreams exhaled,
Sounds of inner death.

Pain escapes, a throaty roar,
Dry eyed, sick creature,
No human understanding,
Foreign the sounds.

Wailing ceases, the body slumps
Still yet goes forth,
Dazed, weary, emotions spent,
Into the day, dry eyes—now cry!

In memory of Deana Marie Steele
1981–2007

A note from Carolyn Bradley

I had asked Sharon if she would want to share any of her writings in this book. She sent me two of them, in an envelope that had an address label with the words "GOD IS LOVE." What a beautiful witness to the faith that she kept and her love that endured through it all!

A Journey of Faith

Written seventeen years ago.

I have a godchild whose name is Sarah. She is a beautiful girl, in her teens, who is kind, considerate, and helpful. Sarah has had a lot to deal with in the last year and a half. Her father, a minister, was killed by a car while trying to help other people on an icy road. Sarah was there when it happened, and of course, the pain and struggle of it all has been a very difficult journey for her, to regain her sense of balance, hope, trust, belief, and faith.

Sarah recently gave a talk on "faith" for her church retreat for youth. Sarah expressed herself beautifully when she stated:
"Faith is a trust we have in someone we can't even see!"

That takes a lot of trust and a lot of faith, but it goes beyond even that. It takes a *willingness* on our part to *try* to believe, and to *try* to trust . . . even though we *can't* see. Sarah's words strike deeply into our own hearts, as we try to examine our own faith, belief, and trust.

Sarah could not believe what had happened to her father and went through a deep questioning of her faith. She questioned God as to "why this had all occurred" and said she was "mad and angry with God." "I didn't trust Him anymore," she stated in her talk, "and I had lost almost all of my faith."

These are heart-piercing words, and words we can all understand. Sarah went on to say that months after her father had passed away, she had gone to a retreat at her church and "was helped by her brother who was one of the counselors there."

She was able to "open herself up to the people that she was with and told them exactly how she felt." She stated that "that was the moment when she first started to feel God working in the people around her and herself."

Sarah received a healing at that retreat, so she decided to speak at a future retreat, to "help at least one person understand themselves better."

Sarah said that "she began to regain her faith in God and that it became stronger than it had ever been." She goes on to say, *"I had a great deal of pain lifted from my heart and it was replaced with an incredible sense of calmness that I had never known was possible!"*

Sarah's pain is *our* pain too, as we think back to that horrible event of her father being killed right before her eyes. But Sarah's joy is also *our* joy of seeing her come "through the fire . . . as pure gold" and of listening to *her* words of comfort for others, encouraging *them* in *their* journey of faith.

Sarah ended her talk with the words "My hope for each of you is that you will begin, if you haven't already, to start your walk of faith and experience the calmness and peace I have found. Don't expect it to happen fast. It's taken me all these years and a great deal of obstacles to come this far, and I know I still have a lot more to learn and understand, but I probably always will. *One* thing my dad always said was

"It's okay to doubt your faith at times, because when you're doubting, you question your faith more—and you eventually come to some sort of answer for yourself, and your faith becomes stronger."

This is her hope for us all—and her *gift* to us all—and a legacy of love that her father is *still* giving . . . through his beautiful daughter Sarah.

(Quotations and excerpts from Sarah Walker
and Rev. Hugh Walker)

Rev. Hugh Walker passed away on Thanksgiving Day, while assisting a motorist whose car had skidded on the ice. He was hit by a passing car, in front of his wife and daughter. Reverend Walker had lived his life in goodness, kindness, and a deep caring for others. This is a note, written by his daughter, Sarah.

A Note for My Dad

Sarah Walker-Haymond

Sixteen years have passed. Numerous birthdays, a graduation, my engagement, college years, my wedding, the birth of my children, my first job, and so much more. All moments and memories that he should have witnessed.

Precious moments that I missed sharing with him. Since my dad passed, each moment, each event has always made me feel one more step further away from him—one more thing he didn't know about me.

This Thanksgiving though, my sixteenth without him, I'm starting to imagine this differently. Yes, I'm still sifting through questions, "what ifs," and difficult days . . . that will never change. However, I'm realizing that all these moments were dreams he had for me. He had probably envisioned many of them, like all parents do.

I go back to a memory I did get to share with him and never really knew its significance until I became a parent. On Mother's Day, my father would get all the mothers in his congregation a flower and present it to them during church services. One Mother's Day in particular, he gave *me* one as well. It seemed silly—I was just a child. When I asked why he was giving me one, he replied,

"For the mother that I know you'll be one day."

At that time, I didn't realize how important that small gesture would mean. He was already celebrating with me a dream he had envisioned. So this Thanksgiving, I'm thankful for that small moment . . .

. . . a moment I'll cherish forever!

Sarah Walker-Haymond wrote this note
on the *eighteenth* anniversary of her
father's passing.

This Thanksgiving marks eighteen years since I lost my father. It was such a long time, but I realize I have so much and so many to be thankful for. I have tagged each person who has helped me heal along the way.

Maybe it was something you said or didn't say. Maybe it was a hug, a single moment, or a lot of things that added up. Maybe it was a reassuring look, or an understanding of where I was coming from. Maybe you are someone, like my husband, who continues to help me daily without even knowing.

Some of you knew my father well, and some of you have never met him.

Whoever and whatever you may have done, I am thankful for *you*!

The Test of Losing a Loved One

Michael Walker

In many ways, the passing of a loved one changes a person forever. I say this with experience. It has been eighteen years since my father passed away. It was sudden and unexpected. He was a minister in Fairmont, West Virginia, for several years. He believed in his church and his parishioners, but most of all, he believed in his family. He spent countless hours at work but even more hours molding me into what I have become today.

Being that he was a minister, I was raised in a religious household. But when he passed away, it tested my faith and hope but made me love my family more than ever.

Faith, in my belief, is one of the cornerstones of what many Christians use to keep themselves from being afraid of what is to come. To this day, the passing of my father has tested my faith. I struggle in the notion that God has His hand in all that happens but yet turn and thank Him when something good happens. Someone once said that God needed my father in heaven more than He needed him on earth.

I couldn't fathom that God needed him or anyone else for that matter, more than me. I believed that His work here was unfinished. I was only nineteen. Who was I going to go to for help? I still had big decisions to make in my life. For instance, how would I know when I found the person I would marry or should I take this job or that job, and have I made him proud?

Although in some odd way, I got through the bumps in the road. You see, there is a thing called hope that is there to guide us and what I believe to be another cornerstone of my Christianity.

It helps give me the strength to carry on. It is the glimmer of light that one may see in the hour of darkness. You could find it in the lyrics of a song or a smile from a friend. It is not, however, *easy* to find.

After losing my dad, hope, as I knew it, was gone. I would say that my family was lost. I know I was.

The one person who taught us how to have hope was taken. In a flash, my world was turned upside down. I knew that having hope could help me get through, but it didn't seem to help. I remembered all the sermons I heard from my dad about having hope, and yet I couldn't find it.

I left town. I ran and I tried to hide from this tragedy. As the years went by, I stopped running and started to let the light in. I knew it was time to settle down.

That is when I found love. As corny as it sounds, I found love. What a word—it supersedes all others! It is the most powerful word that God gave to us.

My father believed it. He preached it not only to me but to many others he was in contact with. It just took me a while to find it. That is what I base my life on today.

I have found that loving my family, no matter what they've done or said, is the greatest gift that we can share. I have a beautiful wife, two wonderful children whom I love with all my heart, a loving mother, brother, and sister.

The list could go on. Losing my father was tough, but knowing he loved and cared for me has given me strength.

Now I know as a husband and a father that what really matters is family and the love that is shared.

It can be tough at times, but love prevails. It is what keeps me grounded and has me waking up every morning with a smile on my face.

You see, I think things happen and we'll never understand why. As humans, we are challenged every day to move forward, to not look back, after the loss of a loved one. It's not that easy. It can make us question our faith in God, ourselves, and others.

It can lead us to places that make us feel lost and unworthy of a better life.

It can keep us from seeing the light that is shining before us, by covering it with shadows. We can miss the words of hope because of the clanging noises that surround our every day. I have been down that road, and I found the solution for me in the love I share with my family.

So when life has you down and out, return to the security of the ones who love you. Take comfort that love is the most powerful gift that we can give and receive.

Share it with those closest to you, and give it to those in need. Loss can take time to heal from, so love the ones that can help heal you through this time.

This is dedicated to my father,
the late Rev. Hugh E. T. Walker.
I love and miss you.

I Rejoice

Marilynn Walker

I rejoice!
For there *is* a light in the distance,
A light that promises Hope.
For so long the darkness
      seemed endless,
But now my soul is renewed
      with life and hope.
I rejoice!

Got Church?

Edward J. Kochman Jr.

The awesome works of God take place on a very regular basis: down the street around the block, more than often on a Sunday morning in a church near you. Lives are changed, marriages mended, and yes, miracles take place.

There is nothing that takes place on a Sunday morning better than what God does in His church all over the world. Some of the best music, the most powerful teachings, and the best of friendships take place in houses of worship.

To neglect or miss these gatherings of believers is a great loss. If you are not a regular attendee, attend. If you do go on a regular basis, get involved. Get to know people. Learn to serve. Find a niche and fill it. Get plugged in. Invest your talents, gifts, and resources. The return will not only be incredible but everlasting.

Come see the works of God in your local church; He is awesome in His doings toward the sons of men.

Pray the Scriptures

Edward J. Kochman Jr.

Lord, may it be as You say. May Your face shine upon those who call on You out of a clean heart. May they see Your salvation and experience Your presence. May those that fear You know You and the power of Your Resurrection.

In like manner, may those whose ways are forward and arrogant fall by their own devices. May they continually stumble until they realize that they need a Savior. Keep the wicked from prospering in their ways, and hinder the perverse from their perversion. May those that rise up against You and Your designated authorities come to their senses and turn from their wickedness.

Open the eyes of the blind, cleanse the mind of the contrary, and convict the ways of the *sinner*. May we pray the scriptures and heed their warnings. May we understand that the Lord does smile upon the righteous but turns His back to the wicked. Above all, may we be the ones You deem righteous not by our righteousness but by the righteousness of Your Son, in whose name we pray. Amen.

A Meditation
The Cry

The cry of Jesus from the cross,
"Father, forgive them, for they know not what they do!" is for us all.
(Luke 23:34)

Father, *forgive us; we don't know what we do*!
Forgive us for our blasphemy, our wrongdoings.
Forgive us for not obeying Your commandments, for doing things on our own.
Forgive us for using our talents, our gifts, in the wrong way.
Forgive us for not listening to Your commands and Your wishes and taking matters into our own hands.

There are many things to forgive—our sin, our doubt, and the misery
we may have caused others—but in all the forgiveness
      there is still love—
      love to the fullest
      for us all.
Help *us* to forgive those who have hurt us—as *You* forgive.
Let *us* say about them,
"Father, forgive them—they know not what they do!" Amen!

Cover the Earth

Come, Holy Spirit,
  Enlighten the darkness,
    Let thy healing rays
      cover the earth with
        softness and light

Come Holy Spirit,
  Enlighten *each* heart,
  Send healing,
  Send truth,
  Send peace,
Cover the earth with warmth,
  all by God's might

Come Holy Spirit,
  You are *one* with the Father,
  one with the Son,
Look in each corner of the earth,
From sea to sea to sea,
Look, Holy Spirit,
  Make all things right!

PART TWO

"I give you a

new command . . .

Love one another

as I have loved

you."

(John 13:34)

A Breath of Kindness

Look and see
All that you *do*
        is *love, kindness,* and respect.
Look and see
All that you *think*
        is *love,* peace, and joy—
        then . . .
        taste and see
All of God's delights
        in your soul—
                forever!

The spaces that we encounter in our lives leave memories that we will never forget.

The Beautiful Spaces

Michael Majoris

Our family living room arrangement remained the same for over a decade, yet a small, hidden section behind a two-seat couch and a cabinet became the setting for my imaginative world of action figures.

An unfinished basement with a used pool table, some seasonal lawn furniture and a secondary refrigerator with Black Cherry soda, and a perfectly imperfect outdoor basketball court with an overhead spotlight were the cornerstones of both our family's recreation and my memorable teenage years. As I entered junior high as a very shy individual, I was fortunate to have instantly bonded with several classmates, who I still have close ties with some thirty years later. Often as teenagers, we think of ourselves as invincible or focus more on trying to outwardly impress others, but within this special retreat place of billiards and hoops, our circle of friends replaced dares and bullish acts with some real deep-down sincerity, truths which aided in all our developments into young men.

Throughout my life, I have experienced many wonderful places or, in more exact terms, beautiful spaces, like the ones from my childhood home. Space is defined as a measurable physical area and can further be described by what is surrounded or located within it.

Nature and the outdoors in all its glory encompass us, filling our senses with many delightful sights and sounds. We have our favorite tree, walking path, or fishing hole. We know the best spot to view the sunset, and we are comforted by the chirping crickets and bellowing frogs during a warm summer night.

In my adult life, whether residing in Buffalo, New York, or Bergholz, Ohio, the external environment has always been there to provide peace and tranquility. Sometimes, I opted for the bold and spectacular, such as Three Sister's Island and its rapid waters, preceding Niagara Falls. Seeing how far I could walk and steady myself on its rocks gave me the opportunity for a little solitude as most folks were stationed in a position to actually see the falls. Other times, I chose a less scenic backdrop but of equal measure. The flat, wide fields at our first, rural Ohio home was a great place to just lie in the grass, bake in the sun, all the while with our Newfoundland dog, Baxter, at my side, my wife planting something, and the kids nearby on the playset.

Space also serves us well in the form of places we visit or attend frequently. It is in these buildings or attractions where special memories and feelings of good will reside. We often find ourselves returning to the place where we met our spouse, made plans to travel to the same vacation spot, fondly recalled a grandparent's home, and shared many dinners with loved ones.

As a father of two young children, I feel blessed that I get the opportunity to share a few of my favorite places as we annually go to the historic Kennywood Park and seek the same thrills in the same roller coasters that I rode in my youth. My wife and I become enamored as we take the kids to where I first saw her—singing at an opera house in Fairview, Ohio—and I am so overcome with joy that my children get to partake in the same Christmas Eve traditions and family togetherness as my cousin has now taken the lead on the dinner, with Grandma still making pierogis at age ninety-five.

Recently, however, I have come to appreciate a less obvious but deeper kind of space, one which is not picturesque and does not contain a special memory but has been there all along. This kind of space is the short passage of time or the quiet rest in one's day. It is the many moments which fall between all of life's commitments, demands, and activities.

We each focus on the "big stuff" in life, moving robotically to school or to work or to other responsibilities and hopefully to a little sleep, and then the cycle begins again. Yet I have learned that often the best part of the day and what helps me cope and persevere are all the little things.

As a musician makes a good song great by instinctively knowing or feeling when a rest in the measure is called for, the many unspoken gestures or actions, sometimes very short, can completely make my day. With the bulk of one's stresses, often occurring at the workplace, it is the warm smile I receive at the beginning of the morning or a compassionate look of support during a turbulent meeting which help carry me forward. Quite simply, it can just be a moment to walk away from one's self, perhaps a trip to the water cooler, to take time to compose and then decide to not send a particular emotional e-mail.

At home, amidst all the chores and clutter which come with young children and pets, the sound of laughter, a spontaneous hug, or a few moments of quietness with my wife on a porch swing are solid reminders that contentment and happiness are paramount.

Daily communication has also been significant. One quality conversation can minimize any ill feelings or hostility which may reside in me. There is nothing better than the natural ebb and flow of a great face-to-face dialogue, where each participant effectively listens, giving ample "space" for the other to turn thoughts and feelings into words.

Often, just being still and listening to the Sunday sermon from a very gifted pastor can make time slow down enough for me to take stock in my own ways and help me to realize God's continuous presence.

Yes, the "big stuff" is not always relegated to the daily grind. There are many celebratory events throughout the year such as weddings, baptisms, and birthdays or that highly anticipated vacation, but as I now reflect on the major events of my life, it was always the small, unplanned, and short-lived moments which have had the most positive effect on me.

In June of 1998, my mother and I journeyed to Nashville, Tennessee, to attend country music's annual Fan Fair. Beyond all the sights and sounds of the fabulous music and entertainment, it was just being together which provided the most profound and everlasting feeling. In particular, during our last evening, we sat in a few poolside lounge chairs at the hotel and just talked. I may no longer recall the details of what was discussed, but the closeness I felt that warm summer night has stayed with me ever since. Four months later, my mother's cancer returned, sending our family into another kind of space—a *confined* space.

Grief, anguish, fear, and resentment are just a few of the deep-rooted feelings which surface during a time of turmoil, taking over, compressing, and suffocating our space. Perhaps these are lessons or trials we are all required to endure, but with *God's good graces*, I have come to learn to value and use *all* my surroundings that He has given me, and He himself continues to permeate with His love.

My spaces fill my heart and mind with wonder, imagination, peace, and joy. They have given me a sense of my own self, instilling confidence and clarity, and as I venture forward, I now have a finer appreciation (and source of strength) in all the "little spaces" which may fall in between but are beautiful nevertheless.

Donna

My sister-in-law Donna passed away at the age of fifty-four from ovarian cancer. She had a long battle with cancer over many years of treatments, doctor's visits, and hospital stays.

Donna accepted her illness in a masterful way. She was always uplifting, and her concerns were for others and not herself. She was a beautiful person, inside and out.

She raised two wonderful children and helped with her grandchildren, teaching them responsibility and making them steady, reliable, and decent human beings in this world that we live in.

Donna had an ingenious way of turning the conversation to the needs of others. She had a straightforward way about her, giving you much needed advice or help in a very practical way, always loving and caring.

Donna had long dark hair in her early years and later cropped it to a shorter length. She had startling blue eyes that seemed to sparkle as blue diamonds. She was of slender build and very stylish in her appearance. She made you think of a "polished jewel."

Donna lingered when cancer returned, battling it again, but then came a quiet reserve, a deep acceptance of her "time to go."

She told my sister that "she didn't know why God wanted her at this time but that she was ready to go if He did."

Her next sentence to my sister was:

"I hope that you can find a job soon that you like."

It was always there—the love, concern, and respect for the needs of others.

She respected God too. Her life was made up of deep faith, her prayers, her faithful church attendance, the prayer group that she belonged to, and her private devotions.

When I would talk with her, her discussions were on her children, her family, and the books she loved to read. She was an avid reader, devouring them especially in her last few years when, with the chemotherapy treatments, she was confined more to home.

She would tell me of the latest book she was reading in between her bouts of sickness due to the treatments.

She was a stalwart soul, ready and willing to do *her* part in this world and always to do her *best*, no matter how hard and painful life was at times.

And Donna, you did!

The Angelic Key

Trinity Majoris

It was early morning. I woke up to my mother making breakfast for me and my sister, and I asked where my dad was. My mom said he got called out to fix a neighbor's furnace that had stopped working during the night, and he wasn't home yet. We had our breakfast and Mom found Dad's set of car keys on the kitchen counter. I said, "If those are Dad's car keys, how did he leave?" Mom agreed that it was strange that the car keys were there on the counter. She said, "Maybe he took my set of keys," so she went in to the living room to get her purse where her set of keys were, and lo and behold, she found her set of keys. She took her set of keys and went to the kitchen to get Dad's set. She looked at both sets in disbelief of what she was seeing. She said to me and my sister, "How did your father leave when I have both sets of car keys right here?"

We were all in wonderment of how this happened, and we couldn't wait for Dad to get home so he could tell us how he took the car with no keys.

When Dad finally did get home, we asked him, "How did you leave with no keys?"

Mom held up both sets of keys, and Dad looked at the keys and said, "What!"

I said, "Dad, how did you leave?" He said, "The keys were in the car when I got in it."

I said, "Where are the keys now?"

He said, "I left them in the car." My sister and I ran as fast as we could to the car to see these car keys and when we got in the car, the keys were gone!

We ran back inside and told Mom and Dad that the keys were gone!

We were all trying to figure out why this happened. Then Dad told us what happened when he got there to fix the furnace.

He said, "I got there and of course went to see the furnace and check things out and see what was wrong with it." The man who lived there had his elderly mother living there with him. Dad felt he needed to check on her to see if she was all right. To Dad's surprise, she had a gun to her head and was about to pull the trigger and take her life. So Dad grabbed the gun away from her and stopped her just in time. Dad talked with her and helped her realize that killing herself wasn't the answer to her problems. She told him about how she felt—hopeless and helpless and like she was just a burden to her son and his family.

When Dad was done, she realized ending her life was not the answer. She lived many more years happily with her family before her natural passing. If Dad had gone back for his car keys, she would have died that day, and she never would have had those years with her son and family. I got to share her birthday party that year with her family and friends. It was a big party, and we all celebrated her and her life that day.

I will never forget that day or the time I spent with this family. Because of the "angelic keys," a life was saved and many others changed, including my own. Because of this miracle, I have an unconditional love and belief in God and his loving angels. On this earth, just ask for their help, and they are there to help.

Smokey

Jim is my brother. His nickname is "Smokey." He was given this nickname many years ago, when, as a young boy, he formed a "Smokey the Bear Junior Forest Ranger Club" for our cousins and friends in our neighborhood.

Jim sent for the club literature, the posters, pins, and the instructions for all the duties of a Junior Forest Ranger. We loved the club. Our meetings were held in a wooden shed in our backyard, adorned with posters of "Smokey the Bear." Jim was the club president and would lead our meetings and activities in promoting fire safety and taking care of our natural resources.

We hung some of the posters in the wooded areas around our houses, and the whole neighborhood joined forces with Jim in his mission. "Smokey the Bear" became a childhood symbol for us all, and we have many fond memories of the club and its purpose, teaching us respect and resourcefulness in promoting good safety habits.

Jim has had other missions in his life. He was faced with a bout with cancer in his early thirties and had to have surgery and then the chemotherapy treatments, which made him very ill. He came through all this with a very steadfast spirit, accepting the day's happenings and then going on to the next. He is a cancer survivor and has been cancer-free for over thirty years.

Jim always had a deep faith, even as a child, and would make visits to our church, with myself and my sister, to pray for the needs of our family, our friends, and the world. His faith was a sustaining part of his life from early childhood.

Jim had other missions in his life, which were to help our parents and his family, which he did with great generosity.

I recently had an illness that was very unusual. I had stinging and burning pains and other strange symptoms that baffled the doctors.

Jim was on another one of his missions to help me, to comfort me, and to bring me hope through the illness. He would call me every day and would tell me that "God is wise and knows what I am going through, and will help me, and that *God loves me.*"

He comforted me, telling me I was going to get through this and that I was going to be all right. His advice for me was to take one day at a time and only think of *that* day.

Jim prayed for me every day, and his encouragement was invaluable.

Thank you, "Smokey." You taught me well. "God *is* wise and *knows* what we *are* going through and *does help* us all, and *loves us all.*"

You accomplished your mission. I *am* getting better, and I *was* able to deal with it, with your great help.

Hats off to you, "Smokey." I love you, and hats off to our childhood hero, "Smokey the Bear"!

God's Grace Is Available

Edward J. Kochman Jr.

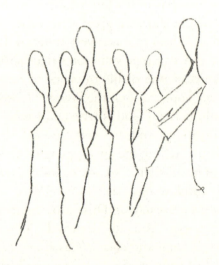

The same spirit, the same grace, and the same power that graced Jesus Christ is available to us.

As Jesus increased in wisdom, in stature, and in favor with God and man, so are we to do so. We have not only those things that were available to Jesus, but we also have Jesus and His word. Therefore, we are to regularly examine ourselves by asking:

"Am I increasing as I should? Am I growing in the grace and knowledge of Christ?"

There is no stagnation in the kingdom of God and His Christ. As a matter of fact, there is no stagnation in His kingdom. We are either growing or we are in a state of atrophy. The only plateau we will ever rightfully reach is the grave.

There is no doubt that the growth of the Christ child came through His obedience to His parents and His willingness to learn. He knew the scriptures and the ways of the temple. He knew His Father through prayer and fellowship.

Let us likewise grow through the realm of God's *grace* and personal *obedience*, being *teachable* with all *humility*.

Regrets

Margie Zellars

"But of that day and hour no one knows, not even the angels in heaven, nor the Son, but only the Father. Take heed, watch and pray; for you do not know when the time is" (Mark 13:32–33, NKJV).

It has been my honor to lead several grief share groups over the past seven years. One of the issues that keep people stuck in their grief is regret. It prevents them from progressing through their grieving process as they are stuck in what I call the "should have, would have, could have" place of regret. If only I would have done what I should have, or if only I would have done this, or I could have done that. Many of us do this looking back on a situation or a time where we could have done more, but this really gets us nowhere. The past is past, and the only thing we can do is learn from these times and let go. Much easier said than done, right?

I live with regret of something I should have said to my favorite uncle and did not. My uncle Sam was such a strong, kind, and loving influence in my life. I was blessed to see him every day as a child growing up as he lived just up the hill from me. We did gardening together, talked about everything, and were just the best buddies there ever was. I look back now and think what a pain I must have been to my aunt and uncle as I was there every day. Before he came home from work, I would go up to their house and set his place at the table, wait anxiously for him to come home to say hello, and then run home as I got my "fix" of Uncle Sam!

On Friday, December 13, 1983, I made a phone call to him that I will never forget. My uncle had severe heart problems for many years. On that Thursday, he was to have a test to determine what course of action they could take to treat his worsening heart condition. On Friday afternoon, I had gotten busy with baking cookies, shopping, and decorating for Christmas, and I completely forgot about the test until about three o'clock. Like so many others, I got caught up in the busyness of preparing for Christmas and forgot to do what I should have done the day before: call my uncle to find out how his test went. When I called, my aunt Annie answered the phone and said that my uncle was having a great time decorating the Christmas tree with his three grandsons, who had come to spend the day with them. She said they were having the time of their lives together and enjoying time with one another. Aunt Annie said that Uncle Sam could not have the test done on Thursday as they found out he was extremely allergic to the dye used in the procedure so they were going to send him to the Cleveland Clinic to do other testing. Knowing that he was spending time with his precious grandsons, I told her I would call another time, but she said no and insisted I talk to him. He came to the phone, and I could hear the joy in his voice as he was having fun with the boys.

I told him I was sorry to hear he couldn't have the test done, but he said, "It's okay because I am doing really good. They'll figure something out after the holidays. I am fine." We talked for a while about other things. All the while I heard this voice in my head, you know that still small voice saying to me, "Tell him that you love him." As much as I had loved my uncle and spent so much time with him, neither one of us ever said those three precious little words—"I love you"—to each other. Funny how that happens; sometimes you take for granted that they know without saying it. Your actions should show it, and you think it's just understood. But is that true? Do they know for sure? Are your feelings truly understood?

I hung up after we talked for about ten minutes so he could go back and enjoy his grandsons and decorating the tree. It dawned on me that I didn't say those three precious words to my dear uncle whom I loved so much. My husband and I went to a birthday party shortly afterward and didn't get home until almost ten o'clock that night. When we got home, the phone was ringing. It was my mom calling me to tell me that at 3:30 p.m., my uncle had a massive heart attack. They were told he was already gone when his body hit the floor. Thank God He allowed me to talk one last time to my precious uncle. It was God telling me to say "I love you" to my uncle. Did I listen to His voice speaking to me? Sadly, I did not, but I am thankful for God leading me to make that phone call and to essentially say goodbye for now. I live with this deep regret that in all those years I never told one of the most precious men in my life, a true gift from God, that I loved him. My hope is that he knew it by my actions.

My message to all of you is to never take someone for granted. It's important to say those words to the ones we love. Some believe you can over-say "I love you." My friends, I am here to tell you that it is better to err by saying it too much than to miss the opportunity to let someone know how much they mean to you and just how special they are. Is there someone you need to say "I love you" to? If so say it right now, today, for we never know when our tomorrow will never come, and we won't have a chance to say those three little words to them. I pose an even more important question to you. Have you told the one who loves you unconditionally, no matter what, that you love Him today? Have you told Jesus that you love Him and thanked Him for giving His life for you so that you may receive the gift of eternal salvation?

Listen to this scripture as found in the Gospel of Mark, chapter 13, verses 32 through 37, as found in the Amplified version of the Bible: "But of that day or that hour not a [single] person knows, not even the angels in heaven, nor the Son, but only the Father. Be on your guard [constantly alert], and watch *and pray*; for you do not know when the time will come. It is like a man [already] going on a journey; when he leaves home, he puts his servants in charge, each with his particular task, and he gives orders to the doorkeeper to be constantly alert *and* on the watch. Therefore watch (give strict attention, be cautious and alert), for you do not know when the Master of the house is coming—in the evening, or at midnight, or at cockcrowing, or in the morning—[Watch, I say] lest He come suddenly *and* unexpectedly and find you asleep. And what I say to you I say to everybody: Watch (give strict attention, be cautious, active, and alert)!

My friends, do not live with deep regret. Let those you love know how much they mean to you. Remember, we do not know when the Son of Man will return, nor do we know when Jesus will come to take us away from our earthly home and take us to the mansion in heaven He has prepared for us. None of us knows when our tomorrow will never come. Do not put off until tomorrow what He is calling you to do today.

Does God Hear You?

Edward J. Kochman Jr

We can pray silently. We can pray while driving our cars, resting on our beds, and working on our jobs. We can pray anywhere, anytime. As a matter of fact, we are instructed to pray without ceasing.

The psalmist uses three inspired words of instruction: "Hear my voice" (Psalm 64:1).

How often does God get to hear your voice in prayer? How often do you verbalize to Him praise, adoration, thanksgiving, and supplication? I'm not talking about a whisper or dinner blessing. I'm talking about conversing with Him "out loud."

I know of no greater way to fellowship with the Lord. Go for a walk with Him, and as you walk, talk. Open up and share your struggles and desires. Ask Him questions. Explain to Him your doubts and frustrations. Then listen with an ear toward obedience.

Afterward, thank and praise Him, "out loud."

Let Him hear your voice.

The Unexpected Gift

Susan E. Wagner

It was Christmas, and the end of the school year was still months away. I'd been teaching a small group of middle-school students in a quaint little town in Texas for three years, but I was retiring. Always one to rise above my emotions and be in control, I wanted no formal goodbyes. But closing the door to my education career and realizing this was the last class I'd ever teach was getting to me.

So, I tucked those feelings away and concentrated on how I could make this a memorable Christmas—one my students would never forget. Wanting it to be perfect, I looked for the biggest tree I could find and all kinds of decorations. When I told them they could even set it up, they were ecstatic. They'd been a close-knit group, always friendly and polite to me. They asked me if they could have a gift exchange, and I said it was okay but insisted they hold the price down to what they all could afford.

With the party in full throttle, I kept thinking about how I was going to get that huge tree with all its decorations home before leaving on Christmas vacation. Just then, I spotted a sad young man with no gift from the exchange. I realized one of them hadn't brought a gift, and just as I began asking who hadn't, he spoke up saying indeed he hadn't. Surprised by his response, I didn't know what to say but knew I had to do something. An idea came to me. Explaining my dilemma about the tree and decorations, I asked if anyone would be able to keep it for me until next Christmas. Not expecting it—every hand in the room shot up. There was never any question in my mind, though, who I would choose—the young man without a gift. The other students were fine with my decision, and when it was time to leave for our Christmas vacation that day, he collected the tree and decorations, thanking me again and again for trusting him to take care of it.

Standing by the window, and thinking I was alone, I stared out and watched him race across the schoolyard holding onto that huge tree, its decorations dangling everywhere as he headed for his home. My heart was overflowing with joy, but suddenly, I realized I was not alone. One of my students had been standing just behind me watching also. Looking up at me, he said, "You know, Miss, he's never had a Christmas tree before because he doesn't have a father, and his mother is very poor and can't afford one."

I'd wanted to give my students a memorable Christmas. They had given me a Christmas I would never forget.

A Beggar

There was a beggar in our little town who used to sit in the little field across the street from our house. It was a grassy field, and sometimes the man, who couldn't walk, would lay on the soft grass or sit upright with a metal cup in one hand.

He would call "hellos" to the people passing by, and he would look at each person very intently, with eyes that seemed to pierce one's soul—right down to the marrow of it. I would hear his cup jingling throughout the day; as we played, some people would take the time to walk over to him and put a few coins in his cup.

I was five years old at the time, and my friends, and my sister and brother and I would play on the sidewalk adjoining the grassy field and have such fun. The hours would roll by, with games of jacks and hopscotch and even roller skating, down to the end of the sidewalk and back up again.

A candy store stood in front of the houses in the back, and it was a veritable child's paradise, to be able to choose at one's will delights of all kinds. There was licorice and gumdrops, bubble gum, hard tack candy, ribbon candy, and caramels fit for a king. Even though most of the candy could be bought for only a penny for each one, unfortunately for myself and my sister and brother, we rarely had any pennies in our pocket to spend.

The other children frequented the store much more often, coming out with their delightful treasures bulging from their pockets.

I would notice the man glancing over at us, from time to time, but he never spoke to us—he only watched our antics and our fun.

One day, however, he singled me out and called out to me, in a clear, sharp voice.

"Little girl, come over here."

While he motioned with his hand for me to approach him. I was a little startled and afraid as he wanted *me* to come, and he had his hand reaching out to me.

I cautiously approached him, and as I got nearer, I noticed there was something in his hand that he wanted to give me. I got closer, and as I did, he reached for my hand and there deposited five shiny pennies in my hand.

He motioned with his eyes then, looking at the candy store, and then gave me a smile, his eyes twinkling as he did.

I understood then, his intent. He must have noticed that I didn't go very often into the candy store, and this was *his* gift to me—five shiny pennies to buy candy, in my hand.

I didn't know whether or not to accept the pennies, as I knew that he didn't have a lot of money, or he wouldn't be there begging every day. But something within me knew that I would be rude *not* to accept his intended gift.

I thanked him wholeheartedly and ran over to the sidewalk and up the stone steps to the candy store. I shared my treasures with my playmates that day, as we all took a break and ate our candy together.

He didn't say anything else—he just smiled at us and nodded his head.

That night, when I went to bed, I prayed for him, as I knelt by my bed.

"Dear God, bless the beggar. Bless him and take care of him," I prayed.

That was *my* gift—to *him*.

One day, he wasn't there anymore. I wondered what had happened, but I never found out.

I still remember the incident though many years have passed. I remember the day a beggar placed five shiny pennies in my hand to make a little girl happy—and he did.

Pennies from a man with a very kind heart.

Pennies from a beggar—who gave, as he was given—despite his plight.

And my prayer will always be:

Bless him, Lord. Amen.

The Glove

Lynda Cross Slowikowski

The boy has grown into a young man
And left behind the toys of childhood
Which now must be saved or abandoned
By the mother who dreads the task.

Trophies and memorabilia are tucked away
Bats, baseballs, bowling balls are kept
In hopes that they will once again be used.
Spikes and cleats are too worn for saving,

Soon the room takes on a new look
One that will welcome the boy for visiting
With only a few pieces of boyhood treasures
Placed strategically about as a reminder of whose room it is.

One thing remains in full view
Although it too should have been
Placed for safekeeping in the deep plastic bins
Alongside the sports trappings of days gone by.

It sits on a shelf in his room
Placed there by his mother
Set aside from the common storage places
Of unused and outgrown athletic gear.

Well broken in from fielding
And the force of balls thrown into its palm
It is a perfect fit for the right hand
Of a teenaged southpaw first baseman

The mother regards the glove
As a precious keepsake
Perhaps because she shares
A common bond with the glove
And that bond tugs at her heart

Both mother and glove share the feel
Of the squeeze of a young hand
As the boy learns lessons in both defeat and victory
With the glove on the baseball field . . .
With the mother in life.

A Christmas Miracle

Mary Evkovich

This Advent, I promised, would be different. Too often in the past, I had been taken up with all the activity of the season and, though unintentionally, felt in some way I had left out what was most important. So I began earlier, much earlier, like the day after Halloween, decorating for Christmas. This was necessary, I told myself, to free up more time during the Advent season. I was quite pleased that it seemed to be working—keeping up with my daily obligations, taking time to assist others, babysitting my granddaughters and stopping at 3:00 p.m. each day to pray the rosary and divine mercy with my husband. Now, I take no credit for this. It was not done by sheer willpower but by the grace of God.

However, as the preparation time for the big Christmas Eve party that we've hosted for at least the past fifteen years drew near, I was starting to feel the stress. On Monday, December 22, my husband and I, sticking to our new resolve to keep Christ the center of the season, agreed to help decorate the church after morning Mass, although advising we could only stay two hours. The countdown to the party was on. I could feel my organizational obsession taking over, estimating that it would take every waking hour until Christmas Eve to complete the food prep and last-minute cleaning.

Deep in the middle of making potato salad, cabbage rolls, and hulushki, with every burner on the stove engaged, it was 3:00 p.m., divine mercy hour—time to stop as promised for our prayer time. But just as we knelt to begin the rosary, the phone rang. "It's Father Manny. I better take it," I told my husband. "Mary," Father Manny began, "the decorating is perfect. Thank you so much." "Oh, you're welcome, Father," I replied. "I'm glad you like it." Then he continued, "Baby Jesus at Sacred Heart (one of the two parishes Father Manny pastors), he is broken." My heart began to race. "Father, I'm in the middle of cooking for Christmas Eve. All these people are coming!" But prompted by grace, I added, "How many pieces is he in?" "Many" Father Manny replied. "It will be a miracle if you can fix him." "You will be like the Blessed Mother delivering Jesus to the world again!" Remembering my own seventy-two hours of labor delivering my son, I was somehow convinced this would be longer. But how could I say no to that? "All right, I'll send Eli. Where is he, Father?" "He is in a box in the manger at St. Joseph Church." "Well, Father, if you want me to fix this, you'd better give me one of your special blessings." "I will pray the rosary for you," he answered.

And sure enough, as my husband entered the side door of St. Joseph the Worker Church, there was Father Manny kneeling like a statue before the Blessed Sacrament in the dim light of the Christmas décor, praying the rosary. Nodding to acknowledge his presence, and pointing to direct Eli to the broken baby lying in a box in the manger, he never said a word nor missed a bead.

"Just buy a baby doll," Eli said as I looked at the infant that was broken in more shards than pieces. But something in my heart assured me that what is impossible for men is possible for God. *If this is God's will and Father Manny is praying for me, it has to happen,* I told myself.

Some pieces gave a clue as to where they might go, but others were nondescript, especially since the statue was painted one gray stone color. With many shards and tiny pieces, I began gluing the first two larger recognizable parts together with my tacky glue and set them to dry, in between stirring the pots on the stove. Six hours later, and after watching as I put two pieces together and then all fall apart for the umpteenth time, Eli gave me a look like "Why'd you get yourself into this?" and went to bed. It was now 9:00 p.m. I was tired and, never being good at jigsaw puzzles, could not figure out what was what. "Blessed Mother," I prayed, "this is the image of your Son. If you want it put back together, you will have to help me! You are my patron saint. I am named for you. Please help me as you always do!" By 10:30 p.m., Baby Jesus was laying on my Christmas table cloth, all in one piece, with the exception of a hole in his head, arm, and back, where pieces had apparently been lost. All of a sudden, the glue had begun to hold, and the pieces of the puzzle were fitting together. Now, there he was resting against a pillow of pine in the centerpiece on my kitchen table. I knew it was a miracle.

With renewed enthusiasm, after morning Mass the next day, I bought the auto body putty my husband had suggested to fill in the holes and a spray paint to match as close as possible. Even the temperature cooperated as I sat in the fifty-degree weather of December 23 on my deck, patching, sculpting, and painting Baby Jesus. Within the hour, there he was, drying in the cold December sun, with no sign he had ever been broken, except for a fine line on his forehead . . . Perhaps in anticipation of the crown of thorns . . . a reminder of the price he paid to make us whole. This Christmas *was* different.

A Gift of Comfort and Joy

Lynda Cross Slowikowski

It was the holiday season, and I was in the midst of Christmas preparations. Then, a text came around 8:15 p.m.: *"I'm in ER. Hurt at work. No big deal, though, promise. I'll be out of here in a few minutes. Will call you then."* It wasn't long before Tommy called to let me know that he had tripped and fallen at work, and his arm was seriously injured. He was to have an appointment with an orthopedic doctor the next day. At that point, everything—the extent of his injury, his work schedule, all his immediate plans—were left in limbo. And that is not a good place to be for anyone! Of course, as his mom, all I wanted to do was hop in the car and drive to be with him! But he said that he didn't want me to do that, and I didn't want to add more stress to his already stressful situation. So I acted on what I believed—I asked for prayer from my church and my friends. Then I cried out to God myself—"Oh God, I know this isn't a life-threatening injury, but he is my son . . . my only son!" Those were my exact words and . . . boom! . . . like a bolt of lightning, those words took on a different meaning. The verse John 3:16 immediately popped into my head—*For God so loved the world that He sent His one and only Son . . ."*—and that one and only Son was sent as a sacrifice . . . for the world, yes, but for me in particular as well. I am not a theological genius, but I believe God "feels" because we have feelings and emotions and we are created in His image. I think that God felt a mixture of joy and sorrow as He sent His Son to earth, knowing He would be the Savior of the world but also knowing the sacrifice and pain He would endure. Being the season of celebrating the birth of Christ, I also had thoughts of Mary. She gave birth, cuddled, protected, and nurtured her child. She knew He was born of the Holy Spirit and was the promised Messiah, but beyond that, she held a little baby boy in her arms and loved Him with a mother's love, raising Him from birth into adulthood. As Tommy's mother, my heart ached for him over an arm injury and what he would have to endure with surgery and rehab. I couldn't help but think about how much pain Mary must have suffered as she watched the Son she loved dying on that cross. We were celebrating the second week of Advent . . . the week of peace. I asked the Lord to give me peace of mind and heart over this situation, and He answered that prayer. I must confess that although I had peace about the situation, it still made my heart ache that my son was hurt and had to go through this rough time. I do not understand why things happen as they do, but I do trust that God is in control, and I trust Him to take what is a not-so-good situation and bring it to good in His time. I claimed Jeremiah 29:11 for my son, *"For I know the plans I have for you," declares the Lord, "plans to prosper you and not to harm you, plans to give you hope and a future."* With joy, I praised God for the assurance that He has a plan for Tommy and was comforted by the peace that passes all understanding that He gave to me that day.

Shepherds

Jesus, shepherds are coming down the hillside. It is the night of Your birth. Their sheep are bleating and their footsteps heard.

Mary and Joseph *hear* their coming. They are coming to see *You*!

Help us *all* to see *You*, dear Jesus.

Help us all to *come*! Amen.

A Visit to the Manger

I tiptoe softly in the stable,
Mother Mary notices me,
She nods and then points to her Son,
"Come, child. Come and see."

Joseph takes his lantern,
Showing softer light—
Upon the baby's face—
And oh—what a beautiful sight!

Eyes that hold secrets from when time began,
Heaven's secrets in a baby's eyes—how can this be?
Eyes that saw prophets and kings long ago—
Open so slowly and then gaze at me.

But what can I say—what can I do,
When heaven's tomorrows are all wrapped in blue?
A love of the father, a love of the son,
A love for all ages, all culminated in *one*.

I love You, I love You,
My heart speaks so clear,
As I gaze in His eyes—
And hold Him so near.

Then, transported in time, to Calvary's glow,
I see a young man, looking down right at me,
Those same eyes, those deep eyes, heaven's secrets for me—
And all my tomorrows—are left on a tree!

The Angel

I had purchased an angel figurine at a garage sale. She was plastic—clear—with a golden trim around her wings, halo, and gown. I had found her in the midst of other Christmas decorations that were all placed together on one of the tables.

She looked a little dull, not very shiny, bright, and "Christmasy," but I purchased her anyway, thinking that she might be useful for the Christmas season.

And she *was*! I learned a valuable lesson with the angel with the golden trim. I placed her in my curio cabinet as I was decorating for the Christmas holiday. I placed her on a shelf with another angel, made of paper mache, who was dressed in gold and bronze that had been there for other Christmases.

A plate with the nativity scene painted on it and a white candle in a golden candle holder completed the picture. I stood back and looked at the scene. It was pretty, but the clear plastic angel looked quite dull and lusterless, like she was stained compared to the other items.

I lit the candle to see if I could see the angel better and the scene was remarkably transformed by the light. The candlelight was shining through the angel's clear plastic wings and gown and illuminated the golden trim with a sparkling beauty. Her face was glowing with the light—making her look ethereal and radiant.

I thought of God and His light. I thought of Jesus being the "light of the world," and I looked at the angel and thought what a miracle God's light is for us all.

For *we* are stained and lusterless, and we need *God's* light, the light of His love, and His grace to transform *us* into beauty, wholeness, loveliness, and respect.

We *all* need the light of God shining upon us, in us, and through us, to make *us* beautiful—*and with Him*—

We *are*!

A Gift of Love on Christmas Day

I cannot give you many things,
A rose would only fade.
A present with its gilt and trim,
Fleeting happiness is made.
But if, within your arms this day.
A wish come true would be,
To lay the Christ child softly there,
And with your eyes, you'd see.
The love, the joy, the constant way,
He watches you with care,
Then all else would suffice to be,
Just blossoms in the air.
For He is love, a love that cares,
So deeply and so true,
That the tiny heart would bleed one day,
And offer it for you.
The tiny brow, pierced thorns would wear—
And over all the cross,
Would be the bed He would lie upon,
And count all things but loss,
If not to gain *your* love for Him,
and *ours*—and *all* who seek,
A better way, a fuller way,
The way to joy and peace.
And that is why my *gift* to you,
on this Christmas Day—
Comes not with ribbons wrapped in red,
But lies sweetly on the hay!

A Star-Filled World

I love stars. They shine in the darkest night—lighting up the sky with breathtaking beauty, serenity, and wonder.

Our minds can't fathom the number of the stars, but we know that they *are* there, and we know that they give evidence to the majesty of our Creator.

There was a star—a long time ago—the star of Bethlehem. It came on a magical night and led wise men to a stable where they found a baby lying in a manger.

"The star went ahead of them, until it stopped over the place where the Child lay" (Matthew 2:9).

We need a star today to guide us to the stable, to the manger. Our world has gone off on its own with immorality, violence, hatred, and a disrespect for life.

We need a star to guide us again to find the Prince of Peace. The voice of Jesus never changes even though some have dulled its sound.

The voice of Jesus calls us to peace, to brotherhood, to service, to caring, to compassion, and to love for all.

Our world needs to hear again the song of the angels in the sky:

"Glory to God, in the Highest, and Peace on earth—Good will to men" (Luke 2:14).

We *can* recover the earth again and make the earth smile again by *accepting* the gift that *has* been *given*, in the birth of *our Savior* and *our Lord*.

Because the Prince of Peace is *still* the King of Peace no matter what else happens.

We only have to *accept* that peace and live that peace in our *own* lives, and then *give* that peace to *others*.

If everyone did that—

What a star-filled world we would have!

A Gift for Ann

My mother Ann was going to be celebrating her ninetieth birthday, and a party was being planned, a surprise party. *All* her neighbors, her *wonderful* neighbors, were in on the plans. They have been so attentive and caring to her all her years living there and also in the last seventeen years after my father had passed away.

The plans were made for a surprise dinner at a dining hall in our town. Her neighbors would attend the dinner and the following festivities. Her birthday is in December, and her neighbors told me they had planned a special surprise—a gift of the Nativity scene to be placed on her front porch that evening when she would arrive home. An arrangement had been made for some of their family members to set up the figures and have the lights turned on when she arrived.

The dinner was wonderful, and my mother had been totally surprised when she entered the room and saw everyone there that she loved, including her neighbors. She enjoyed the celebration, and it was a beautiful evening for her, filled with love and devotion for all her many years and for the beautiful person that she is.

Saying her goodbyes at the restaurant, she entered my car, and I proceeded to drive her back to her home.

Amazingly, the "surprise" was even given to me. We pulled up to the curb, beside her sidewalk, and yes, there *was* the most beautiful manger scene on her front porch. Mary, Joseph, the infant Jesus, and a shepherd and lamb were lit up with a soft glow—a holy glow—and it seemed ethereal.

Then out of the mist, they came, walking slowly, carefully, down the hill beside her home, off to each side, in each direction—her neighbors came.

I looked up, and I thought what a beautiful scene that was. They came like the shepherds, they came like the wise men, following the star to the manger, to see the infant king.

A hush fell over everything, and the scene seemed too holy to even speak, and I thought to myself, as we all looked at the manger, given as a very special gift—

They came for my mother—

And *Jesus* came for us all!

It *was* a birthday she will never forget—
and neither will I!

There Is a Light

There *is* a light in knowing
       God *is* there—through all.
There *is* a light in *believing*
       God *cares* through it all.
There *is* a light in loving
       God and all others,
bringing peace and happiness and joy.
There *is* a light in reaching in the darkness
for a hand to hold—
       the hand of God,
And there *is* a light opening heaven's
       door for us at the end—
to know there will not be darkness,
but *light* at the end—
          Forever!

A Girl of Nineteen

As the girl of nineteen,
Danced in the town hall,
He entered the door,
And saw her above all.

For all he could see,
Was a girl of nineteen,
Swaying to music,
With a sweet tambourine.

He approached her so softly
And asked her to dance,
And thought to himself,
Could this be perchance?

The love of his life,
And the hope of his heart?
And he wished from that day,
They never would part.

He lifted softly her feet
in the air,
And she said that he said,
He always would care.

She said that he said,
She'd never grow old,
She said that he said,
His love was untold.

For the girl of nineteen,
Would be his sweet wife,
He thought to himself,
For the rest of his life.

For the love in his heart,
Blossomed that day.
And the wedding day came,
Not too far away.

And the babies they came,
And the rocking chair rocked,
And all these memories,
Were in their hearts locked.

And the children they grew,
So straight and tall,
And the years drifted by,
With them loving them all.

Then came the middle years,
Autumn's slow step,
She was a grandma,
And like babies they slept,

Right in her arms,
On an old rocking chair,
And she said that he said,
Her face was still fair.

Then came the silver threads,
Binding the gold,
Hands were unsteady,
But she never grew old.

For that girl of nineteen,
Still lived in his heart,
And she said that he said,
They never would part.

She walked more slowly,
And he saw her there,
A girl of "nineteen,"
On an old rocking chair.

Then one day it came,
That the rocking chair sat,
Still and forlorn,
With just an old man's hat,

Crowning the top,
Of the spindles so fair,
And he couldn't bring himself
To sit in her chair.

For she went ahead,
To make him a place,
So cozy and warm,
Filled with heaven's dear grace.

And there she would wait,
That fair girl of nineteen,
Waiting to see him,
Holding her sweet tambourine.

Trust and Fear

Trust is the only way to vanquish fear.
Trust brings *love* and *love* conquers *all* fear.
If we pray to *trust* and *love*,
      fear *will* be defeated.
Fear will leave and it will lose
      its power over all . . . Forever!

I pray to trust and love,
      Father, show me the way. Amen.

The Poor

Jesus, help the poor—
Help them to be gifted lavishly by
all who can help.
Let there be an outpouring of
great love for the poor, and
may everyone do their part in
loving, caring, and helping them.
May the poor be blessed and
helped over all of the earth. Amen.

Little Guy

Barbara Hervey

One day, many years ago, I was walking in my yard. I heard a noise and noticed a baby bird on the ground. It had probably fallen out of the nest. I had a choice to leave him or nurture him. As I stood there for a while, it seemed the Lord was directing me to "try to save him."

I was in between jobs so I had the time, and I figured he would turn out to be a beautiful "blue jay." Days passed, and I fed him baby food, water, and whatever I thought he would eat. I kept him in a box with some old towels.

He grew, developed his feathers, and we named him "Little Guy"! Then I got a part-time job. What was I going to do with him? Well, I took him to work and kept him in the bed of my truck. I went out every few hours to feed him. Eventually, I brought him inside to one of the back rooms.

He grew. Soon it was time for him to learn to fly. My husband Tom and I would put him in a low tree in our backyard and coax him to fly. Eventually he did.

Our "blue jay" had turned out to be a crow, and we were very attached to him.

I would call for him to come back each time he flew, by calling his name, and he would land on my shoulder.

One day, he did not come back. I prayed that he would be okay. I called for him for days, and still no "Little Guy."

After a time, thoughts of him diminished, and I got a full-time job—but at times, thoughts of him would resurface.

So today, when I see crows, I like to think they are descendants of my "Little Guy."

So the day I picked up that shivering featherless body, I knew the Lord wants all of us to "take care of His creatures, both big and small."

First

Father, I am wondering why we do not see *You* first, when we need help. We see everything else, but You.

Then we are lost for a time, until we realize this. Help us to see you, first.

Amen.

Transformed

Jesus, look at us.
See the pain,
        the suffering,
        the bewilderment.

Jesus, make all things new.

(Revelations 21:5)
Amen.

A Rainbow

As a young mother of three small children, I was heavily burdened by a tragedy that had happened in our extended family. The sorrow and pain of this event left me bewildered, saddened, and depressed. My heart felt such pain and hopelessness that I didn't know where to turn. I tried, for the sake of the children, to put on a "front" for them, not allowing them to see the deep pain that I was enduring.

I sought out help from the Bible and would kneel by my bed and read Psalms, raising my hands in praise to God as the words were recited.

"Thus will I bless You all my days, lifting up my hands, I will call upon Your Name" (Psalm 63:4).

I prayed, I cried, and tried to keep verses from the Bible engrained in my mind, for solace and comfort.

"Why are you cast down, O my soul? And why are you disquieted within me?

Hope in God; For I shall yet praise Him, the help of my countenance and my God" (Psalm 42:11).

These verses brought me comfort, but there was still a void in my heart—an empty space due to the devastation of the tragedy.

I went through the motions every day, doing my daily duties, but a part of me was always dwelling on the pain, heartache, disillusionment, and hopelessness of the situation.

Finally, one day came hope. I was at a baseball field in our town, where my older son, who was eight years old, was playing. I had taken my other two children for a little walk in between the games. We came to a little clearing, a grassy spot, where they could play for a short time.

Suddenly, to my amazement, a rainbow appeared slowly and perfectly. It had been an overcast day, with a hazy mist, and a few slight rainshowers, stopping and starting up again. I hadn't noticed the sunlight, but there in the field *was* a rainbow, and one of the ends of that rainbow was actually there on the ground, a few feet from my gaze!

As I walked toward it, it would move farther away, but it *was* there, the *end* of a rainbow that was in so many songs.

There wasn't a "pot of gold," as the song says, but there *was* a "pot of gold" in my heart. I felt lighter, happier, and more contented. God had given me a special *sign*, a sign of *His* love, care, help, and peace.

The circumstances hadn't changed yet, but my heart did, and I knew that things *would* be different now. I would adopt an attitude of trust, faith, and hope, not by dwelling on those circumstances but by keeping my thoughts where they belonged, in the *trust* and *mercy* of God, and in *His* help in the tragedy.

God had brought me *hope*, and I kept that rainbow in my heart—living my days in a lighter way, a happy and more peaceful way—knowing that it wasn't myself that was in charge—but God!

I knew that things would get better someday—*and they did*!

A Grasshopper on My Teacup

Let us walk in the light that God gives us

With all the hustle and bustle of the day's happenings and duties, one day, I decided to treat myself to a time, sitting on our deck in the sun, with a cup of tea.

The tea was ready, and I sneaked out the door so our beagles wouldn't hear me—and out I went to my "time in the sun."

I positioned myself perfectly on one of the rocking chairs, with the teacup nearby, and was ready to enjoy my brief interlude.

Looking around, I thought, *What a day!* The sky was bright blue, setting off the leaves on all the trees surrounding our property.

There were beautiful trees—sunlight captured on random leaves— and the blue sky overhead. It was a sight for a painting!

Suddenly, my picturesque time was interrupted. I began to be bombarded by different insects of all types, flying through the air, some of them like little dive bombers going past my head and circling around me. Other flying insects tried to land on my legs or wanted to choose the very seat that I sat upon, for *their* resting places.

The topper came when I went to reach for my beautiful blue-and-peach teacup, which I had chosen for the occasion, and a grasshopper had just landed on its rim. I was horrified as somehow the tea had lost all its savor to me—and there would be no tea for my "few moments of enjoyment."

I looked around at the scene, noticing the sunlight again, sparkling so beautifully on some of the leaves. I took note of how the shadows on the trees actually made the leaves that *were* tipped with sunshine actually brighter and more beautiful.

I thought of the shadows and hard times in our lives, which somehow make coming through the storm with our heads held high even more meaningful and beautiful when we live through the sunny days of our lives.

I looked around and noticed one section of the trees in the distance had a misty effect; a greying mist seemed to encircle them. I thought to myself that the mist isn't really there. It just looks like that, giving the trees a lighter greyish cast, because they were farther away.

I knew if I went walking in that area that as I walked, the mist would disappear as I got closer. I thought of our anxiousness for the future, our worries, doubts, and fears, and the "what ifs" that plague all of us.

When I thought about it, I saw how the mists *will* disappear there too, for us all, for we have *God with us* at *every* step, at *every* turn in our lives.

The "works of God *are* manifold" (Psalm 104:24), and we need never fear the future for the Lord of all creation lives with us now—and *will* be with us in all our future times. As we walk with Him, hand in hand, the mist disappears from our view—for we are *never* alone.

The time on my deck didn't achieve my desired results of rest and relaxation and a cup of tea, but I thought how even in life, when we think things have gone wrong, or not as we would have liked, a little "jewel" of the day may be found hiding for us to find and to keep always.

I didn't get what I thought I wanted, but I got something more. I hope you do too.

The memories we give our children and grandchildren last forever!

A Memory to Keep

Colleen Mindzak

Isn't it amazing how a simple song playing on the radio can instantly transport you back in time? I had heard a song about being on a high hill, and in a moment, it took me back to such a special day. It was my birthday, and I was six years old—it was a wonderful day!

It was the height of summer, a perfectly clear day, and we were entrusted to his care, that afternoon. John was his real name, but my brother and I called him Jezdo—that meant "grandfather" in Slovak. Jezdo had my hand in his, as we climbed higher and higher. What a steep climb it seemed to be, and I couldn't even imagine what we were about to see. It was a new adventure for me, but not for grandfather, as I would soon learn. He knew exactly where we were going, and when we reached what I thought was the top of the world, he guided me to the biggest stone I ever saw. This stone had a natural blanket over it, as it was covered in a fine velvety green moss.

As I sat down, there it was in all its splendor and majesty—the whole entire world seemed to be displayed before us. We could smell the wonderful fresh air of summertime and see the beautiful colors of the earth at its prime, with flowers blooming everywhere. The entire town could be seen from this height—the cars driving by, people walking to and fro, children bouncing a ball down the street, lots and lots of homes, and the mill running in full operation.

I knew this sight would forever be engraved upon my heart, and just when I thought it couldn't be a better birthday, I saw my grandfather emerging from a little clearing—the best was yet to come. He brought my brother and me the most refreshing, cold drink of water I had ever tasted. He took us to the spot to see water running freely and told us that in the "old country" where he came from, there were many such springs where people came with jugs to get water.

Sometimes, when I want to have a special moment, I think of the big stone covered in fine green moss, and in an instant, a part of heaven opens before me!

A Family's Gift of Prayer

Bernadette Finley

One of the fond memories I remember and carry with me from my childhood is praying the rosary together as a family. Each evening, after my dad came home from work, we would kneel around my parents' bed and say the rosary before supper.

A priest who was a friend of the family had given each of my sisters and brother a pair of rosaries. My rosary was purple with heart-shaped beads and a beautiful cross and medal of the Blessed Mother and Jesus.

My parents taught us all about Jesus early in our lives. Their godly influence made a huge difference in us. Our minds and hearts were so filled with God's love. God was a very important part and member of our family. He could be felt, heard, and seen with the eyes of our faith every day in our home.

The rosary made our family feel so close and helped to keep our hearts humble with the knowledge of how great the kingdom of God was.

My dad had a sign hanging up in our kitchen that read:

"The family that prays together,
stays together."

It was at this time I developed a real devotion to the Blessed Mother and loved to say the Hail Mary prayer. I remember looking lovingly at pictures of Mary in our home, realizing how beautiful she was and how wonderful it was that she was Jesus's mother.

I felt that through praying the rosary each day, I began to connect on a deeper and more intimate level with her Son, Jesus. My relationship with Mary had brought me closer to her Son, Jesus.

As I grew up and married and had children of my own, I felt it was such a beautiful privilege that was given to me as a mother to teach my children about God and the rosary.

Bernie

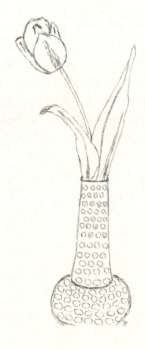

I have a friend, and her name is "Bernie," short for Bernadette. Bernie loves people, and people love her. She is an amazing woman. I call her an "angel on earth"—*and* she is. She has helped so *many* people, giving of her time, her skills, her talents, and her energy. She thinks of others before herself, always caring and inviting, thinking of what *can* be done to help a situation, to bring comfort, hope, and peace.

Bernie is also a registered nurse. She has helped many people through her nursing and by taking care of the elderly in their homes.

Bernie is a steadfast woman of prayer, but she doesn't leave it at prayer. There is always a call to action also. She is always there, loving, caring, and sharing her good wisdom, her quiet trust, her sound advice.

The list of people she has helped is amazing as she continues on, in her daily work, feeding the poor, her involvement in church activities, and her prayer groups.

Bernie's arms are full of loved ones whom she has tenderly cared for with the utmost devotion and respect.

She never indulges in malicious gossip or unkind words. They are not a part of her vocabulary, even when hurtful words might be spoken to her. She is an example for us all, of truth, dignity, respect, and love.

She is above all kind—kindness emanates from her as from a holy stream.

She is like the godly woman spoken of in the Bible "whose worth is beyond rubies" (Proverbs 31:10).

She brings light to *her* part of the world through her decision to *be* light for others.

I know a real angel *did* come to earth.

Her name is "Bernie," short for Bernadette.

Peace

Peace is quiet love,
      Love that rests.
We need to rest
      in God.
He is all quiet.
He knows there *is* a way.
The way is *truth*.
God will show the way,
      if we ask.
Father, we *ask* for peace.
We ask for truth to be made
      known in our lives.
We *ask* to see *You in* our lives,
      working all things for our good.

Amen.

Father's Gifts

A pirate ship, a castle fair,
A boat to take us everywhere,
Our swing became these every day,
The swing my dad made for us to play.

We had such fun, we laughed and played.
No children could have something finer made.

We were rich beyond our wildest dreams,
With the two swing seats,
And the wooden beams,
That carried us to places rare,
And made our hearts so free from care.
On that swing I could never be sad,
The swing so wonderfully built by my dad.
There were other gifts and inventions rare,
And He did these all with love and care.
And that's why I think of "Father's gifts,"
And *all* the gifts they give away,
For all the memories of these gifts,
Will always be in our hearts to stay.

And since heaven's a place where *dearest* wishes come true,
I know up there in heaven's blue,
Just around the bend, I expect to see,
The swing that my dad made for me!

> I love you, Dad,
> Carolyn

Balloons

I had gone to a variety store to purchase balloons for my granddaughter's birthday party.

After selecting the ones that I wanted from the samples, the clerk immediately went to the boxes where the flattened balloons were kept. She selected each one that I had chosen and tossed them onto the counter, and as they landed, they made a sound of dullness and flatness.

I looked at the balloons lying there, and it reminded me of how our lives can be flattened, dull, and without a spirit of joy when *we* are missing something, and that something is the gift of the Holy Spirit, to breathe life—true life—and joy into our hearts, souls, spirits, and bodies.

The clerk carefully attached each one to the helium container and within seconds, they were "life-filled," soaring beautifully, attached to multicolored ribbons and secured to the weights.

I thought of our lives. We can be flattened, lifeless, weighed down with many doubts, fears, despondencies, and depression. We can be stuck in the mire of self-pity, degradation, and despair.

To revitalize and make our lives new, rewarding, fulfilled, and spectacular, we need an indwelling of the Holy Spirit in our hearts.

We need a wind, a breath of God, to breathe into us wholeness, beauty, and respect.

All that we have to do is *ask*!

The Feather Quilt

I had an aunt who showed me the real meaning of the word *hospitality*. Being out of town for a funeral in our family, my aunt invited my mother and myself to stay overnight at her house. We accepted her gracious invitation, and from that moment, we were treated with the utmost consideration.

My aunt immediately began to busy herself with getting things organized for our comfort. Hurrying and scurrying in the kitchen, she soon set a delightful snack before us on the large wooden table in her country kitchen. Her kitchen held the wonderful aroma of good foods that had been cooked there for years, and I eagerly sat at the table while watching my aunt.

Her eyes glistened as she made plans for our night's lodging, as she tried to decide where she thought we would be the most comfortable. She settled on the fact that my mother and I would sleep in her room, and she wouldn't take no for an answer.

Going to bed that night was a treat, as I spotted a huge feather quilt laying across her bed. It was chilly in the upstairs rooms of those old country homes in those days, and the feather quilt delighted my eyes.

It was only minutes later that I was being tucked underneath the quilt, and my aunt was checking the room to make sure everything was just right.

After she had left the room, and we had put out the light, we heard a slight tap on the door. My aunt entered the room, saying, "I forgot to kiss you good night," and she gave me a kiss on the cheek.

Tucked under the feather quilt that night, I thought of her kindness and how she didn't seem inconvenienced at all by our stay. Coping with the death in our family was traumatic, and she had made everything easier by her hospitality.

As I grew up and had my own family, I have often thought of that feather quilt and the lesson that was taught to me by my aunt. She showed me the real meaning of hospitality and how important it was to make people feel at home and comfortable.

I never told her the valuable lesson that she taught me, and I wish that I had. We all need a "feather quilt" in our lives at one time or another, and we are truly blessed by the people who give us one!

One More Ride

(Written fifteen years ago)

We recently took our little grandson Corey to an amusement park. What fun he had going from ride to ride—his whole face beaming with joy and delight. It was his first time at a park, and after each ride, he would look up at his mom and dad and ask, "One more ride?"

It was such joy to see *him* so happy and thrilled, that *our* hearts were totally immersed in giving him this happiness. I noticed other families doing the same thing with their little ones, and I thought of how good God the Father must feel to be able to delight *us* in the same way.

The love that we feel for our children and grandchildren comes from the heart of God. We learn this love from Him, and it is He who teaches us how to care for and give love to our little ones.

We are *all* God's "little ones," and I could picture Him standing there at the amusement park and delighting in *our* delight. I could "see" Him watching *our* faces for signs of joy and happiness as *we* watched Corey's face around every turn, to revel in His sheer delight. God is a good God, and a loving, caring, and forgiving God. He forgives our wrongdoings when we repent, and He gives us many opportunities to receive His joy and blessings.

God *loves* to bless, as stated in the Bible: "If *you* know how to give good gifts to Your children, how much more does your Heavenly Father give good things to those who ask" (Matthew 7:11).

He is a *giver* of gifts—a "*blessing* God" who wishes to give and give and never stops giving all His delights to His children.

Corey couldn't believe that there was still yet another ride for him as we toured the park that day. I can picture our life on earth and especially the eternal joys of heaven as an "eternal amusement park" where all of us look up to God and ask the same question Corey did—"One more ride?"—and of course, the answer is *yes*!

To a Hummingbird

You stopped to pay a visit
to my flowers there.
You didn't stay too long, I know,
But I felt God's care.

The day was ruffled with worries and toil,
My heart was in a whirl.
But then I saw you grace my flowers,
And the day became a pearl.

Within my heart there lives today,
A priceless gem, a jewel rare,
For you graced my porch
and softly stayed,
To lift me full of care.

O little hummingbird,
I do not think you see,
What you did this precious day,
For both God and me!

For in my heart,
You will always stay,
Throughout the moments,
of each new day.

Little hummingbird,
Do you know?
You came for a moment,
But I will *never* let you go!

A Mother's Prayer

Father, help me to be a good mother. Motherhood is such a big responsibility. I am given charge of another human being. I am given a *life* to guide, to nurture, to respect, to care for, and to love all *my* life.

Father, help me to do *my* best and help me to ask for *Your* help in *all*. Father, show me the way! Amen.

A Father's Prayer

Lord, help me to be a good father to my children, to offer them a safe, secure home—a safe, secure life. Children learn from their father many things.

They learn to trust, to be themselves, their very *best* self, and to lean on him for guidance and strength.

Help me to measure up to their dependence on me, that I may use Your wisdom, Your comfort, Your strength for them each day.

Amen.

Blessing

Jesus, the world is crumbling,
It is a sick world,
Help it to be well,
      well with freedom,
      liberty, love, peace,
      joy, and happiness.

Jesus, raise Your hand in blessing
over *all* of the earth.
Let the blessing dissipate all
greed, envy, jealousy, and despair.
Let Your blessing go into *all* the
corners of the world,
bringing new life, help,
comfort, and solace to all.

Jesus, make the world shine
      with Your blessing.
         Amen!

A Child's Prayer

Father, I love you—take care
of me, bless me, help me to
always do good.
Help me to be kind, loving, and
      obedient.
Help me to live my life
      with You—forever. Amen.

A Prayer for Our Teenagers and Young People

Kathy Nagy

Dear Lord,

Help our teenagers and young people today . . .

Realize that they are made in Your image, and each has been created to bring You glory in what they do and how they act.

Help them not to compare themselves to others but to be the *best* of who they are, and to use their God-given talents and abilities to help others.

May they never bully someone for their weaknesses or for how they look. Give them courage to learn to pray for those who hurt them instead of "getting even" because only You can change someone.

Calm their hearts to stay on the right path and avoid the use of drugs and alcohol. Help us as parents to teach our children that practicing abstinence before marriage is a beautiful thing and not something to be ashamed of. Deter those who are "on the wrong path." May they admit their fault and seek a trusting adult and the help that You will provide for them.

Help them, dear Lord, to be obedient to Your will and to fulfill the beautiful dreams that You have planned for them. Help us as parents to have wisdom to teach our children respect. Amen.

Send the Wind

Send the wind of Your
     mercy
Oh God—
over all the earth.

Send the wind of Your
     grace
Oh God—
over all the earth.

Send the winds of kindness,
     respect,
     forgiveness, and
     joy—
over *all* the earth.

Come, Spirit, come!

PART THREE

"Grow in the

grace and knowledge

of our Lord and

Savior Jesus Christ."

2 Peter 3:18

Sheltered

We all need to be sheltered,
    safe, and secure.
God is our refuge and our
    strength—an ever present
    help in trouble. (Psalm 28:7)
God *is* our help—in all.
    Father, we give You all—
    all our lives, past, present,
    and future.
Shelter us in Your arms—
There we will stay—forever!
God is our place of safety—
We are *safe* in *Him*—
Come, God—take care of us—
    Now and forever!

Dawn Sits at My Window

When I was a little girl, I remember sitting on the soft bench in our kitchen and looking out the window that framed a picture of our little town. I would gaze up at the bright blue day, or the windswept sky, soaked with rain, or the snow falling in swirls from the sky. I would see a part of the rolling hills that encircled our town and some of the company houses, all in stately rows, each one having a story of its own— and I would look and dream and love and hope and wonder.

I have always been a "dreamer"—and still am.

Growing up in a little coal-mining town in Western Pennsylvania in the 1940s and early 1950s, my heart looks back to that little girl there, and all her hopes, fears, and dreams.

I did dream about being a princess, as most little girls do—and I dreamed about becoming a teacher one day, writing books, and having a wonderful husband and beautiful family.

As I played with my paper dolls, I would reenact family times, going to school, dating, getting married . . . and of course, living happily ever after. My paper dolls were very important to me, and I would keep each set safe and sound in shoeboxes that my mother had given me.

I had movie star paper dolls, bride-and-groom paper dolls, ballerina paper dolls, and small children, with beautiful outfits, to complete the family. I would play with these for hours, and they were a treasured part of my childhood.

When my mother would go shopping in the larger town nearby, she would always bring me a new set of "cutouts"—and how I waited expectantly, to see which ones she would bring me, and how delighted I was with each one.

My mother is a beautiful woman and gave me security, love, motherly care, and a profound faith in a wise and loving God.

I adored my mother and still do—she has been a lifeline for me in her strength, her purpose of living, and her quiet confidence in Jesus as her Savior.

My family consisted of my sister, who was three years older than me; my younger brother, who was eighteen months my junior; and my father, a coal miner, who had worked in the mines from the age of ten. He had to quit school when he was in the fourth grade to go to work to help his family.

My mother worked very hard, cooking, baking, making our clothes, heating up water for our baths (as we had no hot water in the house), and making our home comfortable and beautiful. Our stove was a coal stove, so that had to be heated up too with chips of wood and pieces of coal.

Our mornings in the wintertime would find us running down the stairs to the warmth of the coal stove and standing on the little stoop to get warm, as we fled the two upstairs bedrooms that didn't have any heat.

We were covered up with "perinas" upstairs, heavy goose down comforters, made by my grandmother, who kept geese for the making of such items. She would place the goose between her legs and gently pluck the soft down from under the goose's neck, and then make the wonderfully soft goose down pillows and warm comforters.

My mother told me that as a little girl, she would take the geese to the little creek behind their house for water and would sit under the shade of a tree and play games with her best friend.

My mother's childhood was very happy. My grandfather treated my grandmother like a queen and was so attentive to her needs. There were six children in the family—three girls and three boys—and they all shared in the household duties. They raised chickens and geese, planted a garden each year, cultivated grapevines, canned and made jelly, baked bread every day, and made their own carpets and rugs.

Years later, as a little girl myself, I can remember the loom for the carpets, standing proudly in their garage, and the bundles of rags nearby, and my grandmother showing me how it was done. I marveled at the beauty of the rugs produced, the colors all blended together into a work of art.

Our little town was sandwiched in by gentle rolling hills and the little creek on the opposite end. It lay in a little dip from the mountain chain, and with the church spires everywhere, it looked like it could be on a Christmas postcard. It seemed there was a church on every street; we had the Catholic Slovak church, the Polish church, the Irish church, the Italian church, the Hungarian church, the Orthodox church, the Methodist church, and the Presbyterian and Lutheran churches all clustered in a very small area.

I can remember the church bells ringing out at different times of the day, and on a crystal clear day, it seemed like they were the sounds of heaven, enveloping the town with God's peace.

The town consisted mainly of row upon row of company houses, all constructed the same for the most part, only all wearing different colors. The little rows of streets culminated in a main street, with a row of shops, the movie theaters—we had two of them—and the business part of town at the end.

There was a large pavilion in the center of Main Street used for entertainment on special occasions.

A drugstore with a soda fountain was at the beginning of the parade of shops, and on an occasional Sunday afternoon, I would walk there with one of my friends, and we would have a cherry soda topped with vanilla ice cream. I remember feeling very "grown up" at ten years old, having a friend to partake in a delightful soda.

We loved going to the movies, and I was enthralled with the movie stars. I would collect pictures of my favorite stars and would love getting new ones. Every Saturday in the summer, my sister, brother, and I would walk down the railroad tracks running through the town and go down Main Street to one of the theaters.

My mother would give us ten cents each for the admission price and then a nickel to buy ourselves a treat. It was our special time, and I will never forget how wonderful that was.

I loved my mother. We used to sit at night, on a hot summer night, on the porch swing, and rock to and fro, while listening to the crickets and katydids and looking up at the stars.

Sometimes, we would talk and other times just soak in the beauty, and her arm would be around me. I loved to be held by my mother; it was the safest place on earth.

In winter, the snow came, and the little town in the Allegheny Mountains received a mountain of snow. It came, and it stayed until the spring thaw, and the yard and our brown-shingled house were covered in whiteness. The snow leaped over the roof in huge drifts, and the yard was impassable without shoveling a path or making a trail for the younger ones. My sister used to "make a trail" for my brother and myself, and we followed in her large boot prints as we trudged through the yard and then to school. The snow lay all around us, and I remember how cumbersome I felt in my heavy woolen snow pants and floppy boots, as I tried to place my feet in her path.

School was a wonderful place for me, and I loved getting new pencils and crayons, and a pencil box at the beginning of the new school year. I would have a few new dresses, usually made by my mother from beautiful materials: red-and-green plaid taffeta, black velvet for the trim around the collar, red gingham for a new jumper, with cotton sateen for the blouse, and different vests with gold buttons to wear with my skirts.

I loved getting new school shoes, which were usually black-and-white oxfords or brown "penny" loafers. It was the custom to insert a penny in the opening on the front of the shoe.

Our school building was a two-story red-brick building adjacent to the church. We were taught in school by the Dominican Sisters, nuns who wore black-and-white habits and wore long rosary beads attached to their waists. I can remember the rosary beads making a soft sound as they walked, which sounded holy and good and true. It was as if they were praying—but were not at the time.

Besides my mother, these nuns formed my faith in school, by telling us about God the Father, and Jesus, and His mother Mary and the saints who had gone before us.

We learned the commandments and were taught how to live a good life, with prayer being a very important part of our lives.

Going to church was a priority in our family, and we attended Mass on Sundays and other special days of prayer and made time even as small children to make our own "visits" to the church during the day to pray for our needs and those of others and the world.

I can remember kneeling there, as a small child, in the quiet of the church with the flickering candlelight and saying my prayers to God and asking for His help in all.

However, the fun of my childhood was clouded at times by many fears about life, a deep-rooted scrupulosity about religious matters, such as a fear of committing sin at every turn and a fear of death and dying.

My father had had many fears, and these were passed on to us. My fear of death and dying was aggravated by someone I knew dying at an early age. My heart and mind would agonize over these matters, causing me much pain and worry.

I knew that God loved me, but somehow the scrupulosity would enter my mind and I was rarely at total rest. It was always there in some way, as well as the fear.

Later, as a teenager, I began to see that these thoughts were not of the Lord's doing but an inward distortion of the reality of the goodness, mercy, and love of God.

The cloud of fear before my eyes can only be dissipated with thoughts of love and trust and hope and joy—seeing reality instead of a false image.

As far as my sense of sin being at every turn, what I needed was *trust*—to trust in the *care* of God in my life and a purposeful way to *serve Him* at every turn by *giving* Him my life, asking for His guidance and protection and to do *His* will for the rest of my life. The fear of death and also loved ones dying can only be dealt with by turning this over to God and asking for *His* help, strength, and protection and to trust in His ways and His benevolent care of each one of us—*His children*.

This did cloud my childhood, but there was always the prospect in my mind of special times that were forthcoming, such as the holidays, and summer vacations, and happy times spent playing with my friends. We had wonderful times in our backyard and played all the games of childhood, with my brother and sister and our neighboring friends. There were ballgames, and "Red Rover" and "kick the can" and "dodgeball" and jacks and board games, all with a magic of their own.

Thinking of the holidays, we kept our Easter celebration very sacred and holy. We attended the Holy Thursday evening Mass and then would come home to the smell of "Kolachi" all through the house.

My mother had baked a whole large container full of these delicious nut rolls.

The aroma permeated the entire house, and the first thing that we did was to lift the cover off of the container and taste the "magic" of the roll.

I will never forget that smell or the delicious taste of those pastries.

On Good Friday, my brother, sister, and I would go to the church for the three hours of Jesus's agony on the cross. I remember praying during those hours and thinking how good it felt to have persevered for those three hours, even as a young child, for we had done something for Jesus.

We took the basket to church on Holy Saturday to have the food blessed, to be eaten on Easter Sunday. The basket was filled with colored Easter eggs, the Easter bread, cooked ham, and Kolbassa and a special "cheese" made out of eggs and milk—*sirok* as it was called in the Slovak language. My mother used to wrap the steaming mixture in a cloth, forming it into a ball. The basket was then covered with a white cloth, with an embroidered cross on it, in remembrance of Jesus's death on the cross for us.

We loved all the traditional food and kept this custom each year. On Easter Sunday, we went to church in our new outfits. I can remember that we always wore hats and gloves, and my mother usually made our dresses, for my sister and me.

Our own Easter baskets were filled with chocolate bunnies, marshmallow chicks, and jelly beans, and always with a chocolate cross in the middle.

Being of Slovak heritage, we observed all the beautiful customs of our relatives before us, for all the holidays.

Christmas Eve was our special delight, known as the "wigilia" or "holy supper."

It was a magical night, when my mother would prepare the delicious pierogis made with potatoes, which we looked forward to during the year, among other dishes.

She would be in the kitchen the whole day, preparing the meal, and then the magical time of five o'clock arrived, and the supper began. We had the special decorated "hoplatky" from the church which resembled the bread for Holy Communion.

They were decorated with special scenes of the Nativity or had angels or shepherds depicted on them in beautiful pictures.

My mother would cut them into round pieces and place these on our plates, to eat, and then my father would trace a cross of blessing on each one of our foreheads.

On Christmas morning, I would wake up breathless and excited to see what Santa Claus had brought for us all. I usually got a baby doll with little dresses for her and an art set, or doll dishes, and board games.

It was a wonderful time in our lives. The Christmas tree was the center of all the festivities, and I would look at it all aglow—the red, blue, green, and golden lights shining on the tree—and shining in my heart to this day.

It was as if my heart had lights too!

We would receive so many beautiful Christmas cards every year and always a very special one from an elderly couple who lived across the street from us. Their cards usually had gold or silver foil around the borders, with beautiful snow scenes or wonderful holiday scenes of golden bells or bright candles trimmed with ribbons and holly leaves and berries. Others had scenes of the Nativity or wise men looking for a star.

I would look at the cards with wonder and delight and think how beautiful the world is, and we were a part of all the beauty and wonder and love together.

I don't know if that couple ever realized the impact of those cards, especially when our family had a very low income and had to focus on only buying necessities. They were a part of beauty in my life, and I have never forgotten them.

Underneath the tree was always the manger. Looking at each little lamb lying by the true Lamb of God, the Son of God, the Savior-Child, I would whisper prayers to Him, telling Him that I loved Him and thanked Him for coming.

I would look at Mary, her face half-covered with a veil gazing down at her newborn son, and Joseph, standing steady and true with his staff—also looking down at the newborn king.

Mary's face was always dimly lit, but I knew what she looked like. I knew her look of love on her face—and I knew how she must feel to hold the Savior in her arms.

Santa Claus and the baby Jesus, a twofold holiday, lights and reindeer and bags of toys and footsteps on the roof, and a sleigh that flew through the air.

A magical Christmas—each year.

A magical time to love, to rejoice, and to know that life is wonderful!

I still believe that life is wonderful—even to this day, so many years later. You see, *love* makes it all wonderful—*love* is the key. There is so much love on earth—and in heaven. There are stars and angels still in the sky, as we remember what happened so many years ago in the first Bethlehem story.

There are sons and daughters to love as well as grandsons, granddaughters, and great-grandchildren.

There are smiles from strangers and smiles from loved ones. There are tiny baby fingers and grown-up hands doing the work of the day. There is the marvel of looking at your children and seeing them grow up and looking at their fine bodies and souls, gifts that could never be bought—eternal gifts of treasures and love.

There is all creation to study and enjoy: the sparkling leaves, the ripples in the streams, the snow-covered hills and the night sky ablaze with stars, knowing that dawn always does follow the darkness.

There are things to do every day, our daily duties, that can always be done with more love, more trust, and more hope.

But most of all is the picture of *God's* arms reaching down and holding us through it all—

 We are never alone

 We have God forever!

wherever we are, there is *always* hope—

wherever we are, we can *always* dream and love and care and pray and take time to think about God, *His* love, *His* care, and that He *is* *with us always.*

So many years have passed since that little girl was looking out that window in that little town, and now, as I look out another window, I know that dawn *does sit at my window—for the darkness has no power over the dawn*!

PART FOUR

"This very day in King David's hometown, a

Savior was born for you. He is Christ the Lord"

(Luke 2:11)

The Light by the Way

There *is* a light by the way,
    It is Jesus.
He stands there—the light
that came into the world,
to banish the darkness,
It is the light of God,
radiating on the *face* of the
    Son of God.
He *is* the "Way, the Truth and
    the Life." (John 14:6)
He stands *by* the way—
Waiting for us to ask Him,
to accompany us on our journey.
He does not force himself,
    but gently waits—
for each one of us to ask.
All of us who walk by the
    wayside—may we ask.
May we *accept* His love—
and let Him accompany us—
    forever!

A Meditation
Jesus

Jesus, You were born one cold night in the village of Bethlehem. You lived and grew up in the little town of Nazareth.

"He will be called a Nazarene" (Matthew 2:23).

Jesus, You walked along the dusty roads going to Jerusalem. All prophets must go to Jerusalem. *All* the prophets died in Jerusalem.

Jesus, You died on a cross, outside of the city gates. Your blood spilled on the ground, the ground of earth.

May this blood *now* save the earth, dear Jesus. May this blood *now* save us! Amen.

A Meditation
The Child Jesus Is Lost at Passover

Jesus, we see Mary and Joseph looking for you. Where are You, Jesus? They are searching the city for You. It has been two days of searching, and they go from house to house, looking in the streets, and in the marketplaces. They look for You—but do not see You anywhere.

Someone suggests the temple, and they go there. Jesus, Your mother is so weary. She is saddened beyond belief. Joseph is steadying her. Joseph is looking at her, *very* worried.

What will happen if we can't find Him? he thinks to himself. *How will she bear this? How will I bear this? Never to see Him again on earth! Oh dear God, my Father, Our Father, Our Abba, help us to find . . . Your Son!*

And then Joseph stops. He stops and looks. He sees You. You are beside the teachers in the temple, but *You* are teaching them! They surround You like they do the elders. They are looking to You to speak. How unheard of: a boy teaching men—*many* men!

Mary gives a sigh of relief. It is a gasp of wonder, amazement, and joy. Joy beyond all telling.

"Joseph," she says, "we have found Him! There He is. He is not hurt—He is well."

Then, Jesus, You turn and look. You see them coming—Your beloved mother and your foster father on earth. You give them a smile, your lips curling in an upward twist.

But Jesus, Your mother scolds You, doesn't she? She says, "Son, why have You done so to us? Behold in sorrow we have sought You" (Luke 2:48).

And You say, "Did you not know that I would be in My Father's house?" (Luke 2:49).

But Jesus, *who is* the *Father* that You speak of? Do you mean the God of all creation? Do you mean the almighty Lord of heaven and earth?

Jesus, You *are* the son of the Lord of all creation. The God, the almighty Lord of heaven and earth *is* Your *Father*.

We do not understand *why* Mary and Joseph had to endure such sorrow and suffering in their search for You, but this we do know.

You must have known when You were twelve years old that You *were* the Son of God.

You knew You were the Messiah, sent to save the world. You also knew the sufferings that the Messiah would endure.

Thank you, Jesus—
       for knowing—
       for loving—
       for accepting *all* of this—
          for *us*—
             Amen!

John the Baptist

Jesus, John the Baptist went about preaching a baptism of repentance for the remission of sins.

(Luke 3:3)

"The voice of one crying in the wilderness,
Prepare the way of the Lord,
Make His paths straight." (Luke 3:4)

Jesus, *we* need *our* paths to be made straight.
We need a voice crying in the wilderness,
    "*Prepare the way of the Lord.*"
We need to hear the voice of John the Baptist again, telling *us to repent.*
Our *entire world* is in need of repentance.
Jesus, *save us—give us repentance for all*!

Amen!

Lambs

Jesus, You saw many lambs and sheep in Your life. They were there when the shepherds came, that holy night when You were born. There were lambs in the fields and on the rolling hills, as You learned to walk.

You saw lambs on the hillsides as You preached and also carried the wood for Your work.

You saw their eyes, looking at You—and You said, "I am the Good Shepherd" (John 10:11).

You looked at them and knew that they needed *their* shepherd to guide them and take care of them—to protect them and keep them safe.

You said we are *all* Your sheep—*each one*. You don't want *any one* of us to be lost. You said the shepherd will go after the lost sheep and leave the ninety-nine in the fold until he finds the one who is lost (Luke 15:4).

Jesus, find *us*. Find *each one* of us—let not *one* of us be lost! Amen.

A Meditation
Be Still

Jesus, You were asleep in the boat, and the wind began to blow and the waves were threatening to overturn the boat.

Your apostles woke You and cried,
"*Lord, save us, we are perishing*!" (Mark 4:38)

You spoke to the waves—
"*Be still*!"
And there *was calmness* and *peace.*

Jesus, give *us* calmness and peace.
Say to *our* souls—
"*Be still*!"
Quiet and soothe our hearts, minds, souls, and spirits.

We do not have to live in unrest, in turmoil, in fear, anxiety, and worry.
You calmed the waters, *you* calmed the storm.
Calm us—by Your *grace*—
by Your *word*—

Amen!

A Meditation
Sin

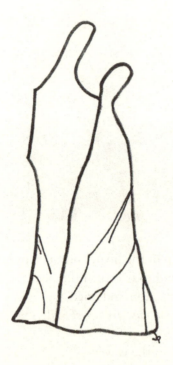

Jesus, the woman caught in adultery
       was lying at Your feet.
       Her head was bowed,
       Her spirit spent.
She was going to be stoned to death.
       You said,
"Let him who has *never* sinned
       cast the first stone." (John 8:7)
       You saved the woman.
       She looks up at You,
           tears glistening in her eyes,
           a look of wonder and relief
           on her face.

You say,
    "Go, and sin no more."

Jesus, help *us* to sin no more.
Our sins keep us chained.
    Loosen the chains.
Free us from all evil
Say to each one of us today,
    "Go, and sin no more!"

Amen.

A Meditation

"Jesus is condemned to death."

Jesus, we see You standing before Pilate. Your head is bowed low. Pilate is talking to You.

He says to You, *"Are* You a king?"

You say, "My kingdom does not belong to this world" (John 18:36).

Pilate looks at You—soul-searching—trying to find the answer in Your eyes as to what *kind* of a king You are.

We look at You. We see Your hair hanging over Your sacred face. We look down at Your feet.

They have walked the dusty roads, and now they will be led to Calvary.

Jesus, do we see remorse in Your eyes for what You know is about to happen? Oh no, there is not—only a quiet acceptance, an unflinching desire to do the Father's will.

You turn and look at *us*—*each* one of us—and You give *us* a commission,

"Go and do likewise—
Take up your cross daily and
        follow *me*.
I will be there with You—
        through it all.
I will never leave You—I am Your Savior."
Thank you, Jesus. Amen.

A Meditation
Glory

Jesus, You will come in glory.
We will see You in the sky.
All nations will see You at the same time.
You will come in majesty and power,
slaying all evil with the
      sword from Your mouth.
You are the Holy *One*—
      Born on earth—to *save* the earth!

You *are* the *Christ*—the Messiah!
You will come with a vengeance
      for all evil,
but with tenderness, love, and
      pity for *all* the good.

All nations will then bend their
      knees to You—

All nations will then call You *Lord*!
You are king forever
        in glory!

Come, Lord Jesus, come! Amen.

Bread of Life

Bread of life,
Shine on me,
In the darkness
Set me free.

Holy wine,
Cup of gold,
Share your riches,
Life untold.

Give us grace,
God's work to do,
Help us always—
See us through.

Bread of life,
Savior of all,
Help us to answer,
God's loving call.

Give us Your strength
Your comfort too,
Help us to be willing,
To do what You do.

Bread of life
Shine on me,
In the darkness.
Set me free!

A Time to Sing

Laughter, joy, peace, strength, hope, happiness, and truth.
Now is the time to sing,
     to sing about God's love and ours.
     God said,
         "Come out from the darkness"—and we can—
         We come out *believing* that He *can* do something.
         We venture out knowing that He *can* help and *will* help
and *wants* to help.
     He lifts us up—up into His *truth*,
     His *reality*, and His *peace*.
     He will do this for everyone!
     He shows us a *new* life, a love, a wonder
     of His beauty and goodness forever.
     It is a life of service and love,
         caring, compassion, and hope.
     We have God—
     We *can* sing—
         and have *peace* in our hearts and souls—
     for the God of all creation
         Loves us all—forever!

He will come with His mighty angels—
    to help—to guard—all mankind.

It *is* a time to sing—
    For the Lord rules—
    the Lord reigns—
    the Lord *will come*
        with victory—
        Amen.

PART FIVE

"Honor the wonderful

name of the Lord

and worship the

Lord most holy

and glorious."

(Psalm 29:2)

My Window

I look out my window every morning. I am anxious to see the "world." My window faces the adjacent yard and the lots beyond which are not cleared but covered with brush and many trees.

I love the yard and the view. Nature works in spectacular ways each morning. The sun wraps her arms around the top of our rose of Sharon tree and then lets her glitter shine on the neighboring trees, spilling over to the grass and bushes dotting the yard.

After the long winter with our frozen yard in view, I woke up one morning to see my daffodils awakening from the moist earth. The dogwood tree was only displaying its tiny buds at this time but was proudly showing me that they *were* there, ready to bloom. Our large pear tree by the house held its snow-white blossoms, which were carefully arranged like miniature bouquets cradled in its branches.

A robin hopped across the yard, pecking her beak down into the soil, looking for a morsel to eat.

I marveled at the sights before my eyes, for indeed, "the winter is now past . . .

> the flowers appear on the earth,
> the time of singing has come—
> and the voice of the turtledove is
> heard in our land" Song of Solomon (2:11–12).

Spring comes in many ways in our hearts, our lives, our dreams, hopes, and prayers.

Spring *is* always there *waiting* to show its beauty, its resilience, and its coming, as we wait for God's purposes, strength, hope, and help in all our situations.

No matter *what* we are going through, the promise of spring *is* there for us all, *in* all, and *through* all.

We have to have the resilience to keep in our hearts the *promise* of spring.

"The flowers *will* appear on the earth."

We only have to wait—and get ready to smell the blossoms!

To Play

The pink-and-white checked liner with the lace trim still peaks out from the white wicker baby doll bassinet in the room upstairs.

It holds three baby dolls—sitting proudly, covered with their blankets, looking at one another and ready "to play."

Many years ago, they waited and were delighted when the little girls were able to play. The little girls were my granddaughters and the play did begin.

We "fed" the babies with the little plastic baby bottle with the pretend milk flowing through the bottle when it was overturned. We diapered the babies and took their temperature with the little red-and-white plastic doll thermometer, and we bandaged their legs when they got a pretend wound. We bathed them in the little blue plastic baby bath tub, and they were clean for the day.

Being a grandmother, I had already played "babies" with my own daughter, teaching her the full gamut of caring for her baby dolls and then, someday, to be a mother of the finest kind.

It worked—and she already had known how to wrap the baby just right in the receiving blanket and tend to their needs.

My house is small, but the upstairs toy room holds a wealth of memories, hopes, dreams, ambitions, and kindness and love all strewn over the items on display.

There are treasures in some blocks in a bin left over from my grandson's days to play, a blue wooden knight belonging to the blocks where castles were made and moats and a drawbridge, as the knight came to save the princess in distress.

There are toy cars—colorful—each in a different design that used to be pushed back and forth by my grandson and his grandfather on the floor in the kitchen, because they could "fly" on the linoleum floor.

There are drawings in the drawers upstairs and coloring books left over from countless hours of using the magical colorful crayons and watercolors to make our pictures come alive with the beautiful colors.

We started coloring when the children were only two years old, and there are their pages with colorful lines drawn up and down all over the pages, works of art to behold.

There are "happy times" still living in that room as I look over the objects and feel the memories.

In the downstairs closet, I still have remnants of my own children's play—the toy gas station, the wooden castle, a boat, an airplane, and the little toy barn that said, "Moo," when you opened the door. Countless hours of playing with my children, my grandchildren, and then, hopefully, my great-grandchildren.

Playing is a necessary, holy, happy time—a time of magical memories that never leave. It is a *gift* we give to *them*—to share special valuable *time with them*, as they grow.

It is also a *gift* we *give* to *ourselves* as well—priceless moments spent with them, in the magical world of playing.

Flowers of the Field

Jesus, You said, "Look at the flowers of the field. They neither toil nor spin, yet I tell you, Solomon, in all of his glory was not arrayed as one of these" (Luke 12:27).

You were telling us to *trust*—to *trust* in Your Father, for *all* our needs.

Jesus, we *need* to trust. We need to be like the flowers of the field, showing the beauty given to us, by God Your Father.

We need to *allow* God to *be* God in our lives. We need to *allow* God to *be* our *helper* and *guide*, showing us *how* to be *trusting, pliable, sharing,* and *caring.*

Jesus, give us this way of *total trust.*

Amen.

The flowers of the field are beautiful, dear Jesus. *We* are beautiful *too*! Amen.

Angel Faces

I get a cozy feeling,
When twilight shadows fall,
And tuck our little house within,
The darkness over all.

The children are bathed and dressed for bed,
And eat a snack or two,
Then off to bed, put out the lights,
And quiet will ensue.

All is safe within these castle walls,
My heart knows deep relief,
That each little bed has a curly head,
And all are fast asleep.

I wonder when they're grown, and gone their ways,
Even though the work will lessen,
How much I'll miss those curly heads,
And know, how great the blessing.

The work, their wants, sometimes a strain,
Their sounds of teasing and weeping,
All fade away and angel faces,
Appear, as they lie sleeping.

And when they're grown and gone their ways,
And the house knows not their traces,
I wonder if I'll tiptoe in,
And look for angel faces!

Looking

What is it that we are looking for?
    It is Jesus.
What is it that we are searching for?
    It is Jesus.
What is it that is troubling us?
    Jesus can help.
What is that hurts us?
    Jesus can heal that hurt.
What is it that calms our hearts
    and gives us peace?
It is the knowledge that we are
    never alone.
We have God at our side—
    every moment of our lives.
What makes our hearts smile?
It is Jesus, loving, caring,
    inviting, hoping, praying
    that we will come under
    His fold—
        that we will allow Him to
        take care of
            us,
            now,
            always, and
            forever!

How to "Water" Your Life

My plants on our deck need watering every day. Languishing in the heat of the day, they "look at me," their soil baked and dry, seemingly begging for a drink of cool, clear water. After they are watered in the cool of the evening, their leaves spread out and upward, their stems glisten with drops of moisture, and they look refreshed and healthy.

We need water—the water of God's *grace*. We are all languishing amidst the heat of the day's worries and trials. We need the soothing waters of His love to nourish, comfort, sustain, help, and heal us. We need the grace of God to flood our minds and hearts, pouring refreshment over our bodies, souls, minds, and spirits.

The grace of God is a wondrous thing. It brings healing to the sick and to those who are sick in heart and soul, as well as their body. It brings strength for the weary, those whose trials seem unbearable. It brings soothing calm to the troubled mind, the mind at war with itself.

God's grace gives us all a new lease on life. It brings a spring to our step and promotes a sunny disposition to our souls. God's grace waters the earth, bringing and restoring new life everywhere. His is a life of love. God loves to sprinkle love everywhere. His love is found in the eyes of babies, and the time-worn hands of the elderly. It is found in the marvelous colors of the flowers; the beauty of the newly fallen snow, all white and sparkling; the softness of a moonlit night; the peacefulness of looking at a quiet lake; and the melodious song of the birds in the early morning, awakening us *all* to new lives.

God's grace is everywhere, and His love is everywhere, spreading the magic of His love over all the hearts that are willing to receive it. This love is a life-changing event—and we are never the same!

We only need to *accept* God's grace, lovingly, openly, and completely to be made whole ourselves, and then we, in turn, can demonstrate this love to others.

Then, we all can bask in the refreshment, as the plants did in the life-giving water that sustains and refreshes us, heals us, and makes us whole!

Getting Even

What is it that hurts you?
Are you crying, bewildered?
Do you want to *punish* someone?
Are you angry?
Are you vengeful?
Do you want to get even?
There is a way *not* to have to get even.
It is through *God's love.*
Give the *situation* to God.
He is bigger than all of us.
He is kinder than all of us.
He is breathtakingly beautiful,
       kind, holy, caring,
       inviting, loving,
       loving *you* with all
       of His heart.
You are *never alone.*
You are in God always.
You are His masterpiece.
You are His treasure,
Yes, you—you are God's creation,
made masterfully,
beautifully, kindly, with care.
You are a creation of the almighty Father.
You have value—far beyond earthly treasures.
You are the *masterpiece* of God, and
He says that you are a *child*—a *child*
of the heavenly Father.
No matter what your earthly mother and
father were like or *are* like,
You have a *heavenly* Father, a Father unlike any other.
Your Father spins worlds, billions of worlds and stars and planets into
space.
Your Father creates thunder and lightning and calm quiet seas.

Your Father created all things upon the earth and upon all worlds combined.

Your Father is the God of all creation, and He speaks to *you* softly and tenderly.

He speaks to you with the love of all the ages.

He says to you, *"Come!"*

> Come to His heart,
> Come to Him—lover of all,
> Come to His forgiveness.
> Come to His mercy.
> *Come, child, come!*

A Time to Be Broken

We are all broken at times.
We all have heartaches, fears,
illnesses, trials, and sufferings.
We all have our crosses—
        each a different one—
        each a different trial—
but God *is* there, *with* each one,
        to *help, hold,* and *heal.*
God *never* leaves us alone!
He is as close as a whisper,
as close as a word of prayer.
God makes miracles happen, for *you,*
for *me,* for *everyone*!
It is in *giving* ourselves to God,
that we *receive* the miracles!
God sees, knows, cares, and loves us
        with an everlasting love.
We are *never* away from His love.
He holds us and graces us with
        His presence always.
When we say, "God, help me"—He does.
When we say, "God, I need You,"
        He is there.
When we cry out, "God, I can't find the
        way!" He is there—to show us
"the way, the truth and the life" (John 14:6)
He has given us His Son as our Savior.
We are *no_longer_broken* when we *give*
        our *hearts* to *God.*
He mends them, restores them,
        and makes them whole.

No matter what has gone before—
No matter *what* is in the future,
God *is*—and *will be* there *with* us!
Brokenness leaves when we say—
    "Heal me, God!"
    And He does!

A Time to Pray

Prayer takes time,
time to be with God
      every day.
Prayer is a matter of the will,
We need *our* will
      to say yes,
"Yes," I *will pray*, today
      and every day,
Prayer is talking to God—
      He hears us each time,
      He helps us, encourages us,
blesses us with His peace.
We need to take time to pray
      Every day—
      saying,
God, we need You—
      we love You—
      we want your help,
your wholeness, your
forgiveness, your mercy,
      and your strength—
Give these all to us, dear
      God—Amen.

A Time to Trust

Now is the time to trust,
to trust in God
for all our needs,
for all our blessings.
Trusting takes time
and patience.
Trusting is a learning thing,
over and over again,
We place our hands in God's hands.
We ask Him to take care of all.
He is there *with_us*—every day
of our lives.
We can safely trust Him with
all.
When things occur—
We need to draw upon our
trust "bank" over and over
again.
We trust because we know
there is *no* reason *not* to trust.
Trusting is the key
to finding peace and comfort
in all the situations in our
lives.
Trusting is the way.
Father, we *do* trust You in all! Amen.

A Time for Roses

I love roses.
They bloom in the summer, bestowing their beauty, their fragrance, and their joy.
It is a delight to look at a rose.
It is a delight to smell its fragrance.
God gave us roses to remind us of *His* beauty, *His* fragrance, and His love.
The fragrance of God is goodness, right, justice, love, hope, and healing.
The beauty of God is trust, faithfulness, caring, love, and peace.
We touch the face of God in each flower, for His spirit breathes in all creation.
We touch His heart when we see Him in all of His creation.
A rose is a symbol of love—love for God—love for our families, love for our treasured ones.
Roses stand for God's truth—
      "I am here."
      "I love you."
      "I will always be with you."
Take a rose and keep it in your heart—a treasure forever.

A Time to Shine

It is a time to shine
It is a time to glow
  with mercy, truth, healing, love,
    and forgiveness for us all.

It *can* be a new world
  brought about by you, me, everyone!

It is a world of *love*—
  Love pierces the darkness—
  Love makes all things *new*.
  Things are made new, beautiful,
  trusting, hopeful by *love* .
  Love makes it all happen.
  Love makes the world shine!

We can be *bearers* of love—
  by loving *everyone*—
We can put love in *every place*—
  everywhere that we are.
We are the bearers of *God's love*!

We need to *forgive* all the wrongs
  done to us—
We forgive the wrongdoers,
  and we forgive ourselves.

When we encounter unkindness—
We can let it go—
  and be kind back—

We can pray for those who are
  misguided.
We can help them change by love.

What a force—what a power—
   Love cleans the earth
   making it shining and new—

And then—the *whole world shines*
   with love!

Always

Father, I love You,
You have always been there for me.
You have blessed me all my days.
You have carried me in Your arms.
I love You, Father. Amen.

Praying

Father,
I pray for all who are sick and in pain.
I pray for all those who are sad and depressed and worried.
Help them, kind Father, in the name of Jesus Your Son.
Amen.

Send Us Light

Jesus, You are light.
The world is in darkness,
>   the world is in such pain.
>   Heal the pain,
>   dear Jesus.
Send us light,
>   love, hope, and peace.
We need *You*, dear Jesus.
>   Bring the light! Amen.

Father

Father, You are good, loving, and caring.
You care for *each* one of us.
You love us.
You are here with us, with your help and mercy.
Father,
>   We are yours.
>   We love You.
>   We serve You.
>   We place our lives in Your hands.
Do with us, as *You will.*

Amen.

Forgiveness

Father, we need to forgive ourselves and
    those who have hurt us.
Help us to see ourselves as others.
You forgive *all*. You look at us,
    everyone!
You see us as tiny souls,
    scarred, wounded, and soiled.
You see *all* the good underneath the
    fear, the doubt, and the sin.
Wash us clean, Father.
Uncover the hurts and heal them.
Uncover the bondage and set
    us free.
Say to our souls—
    "*Be free*!" Amen.

We *need* to be free to love,
    to care, to serve.
Make us free! Amen.

Being Open

Father, we need to be "open" in our souls,
free from all that would make us tight,
    rigid, and afraid.
Being open makes us happy, glad, and content,
    not clinging to fear anymore.
We need to love *You*, giving You free rein
to do all that You will with us.
Being open frees us from our cares, and
    allows us to *look* at *You*,
    and know *who* You are.
    You are kind, caring, and inviting.
    You are pure, holy, serene, and majestic.
Father, *never* let us hold on to fear,
self-pity, doubt, anger, and mistrust;
Father, let us let them go,
    as we open our hands—
    and let them be gone—
                forever!

Life's Direction

Father, You are life. Teach us *how* to live. Give us *Your* life. Give us a part of *You*. Then we shall be safe. Our lives *can* be destroyed through fear, self-pity, depression, and *not* loving. Make us to be calm in You. Give our lives meaning, direction, and purpose. You are the butterflies, the wind in the trees, the flowers, the birds, and the hills. You are a part of *all* of creation, for *You* are the *Creator*!

You are the *direction* for everyone's life, if only we *allow* it. We *need* You, Father. We *accept true life* from Your hands. We accept the *praise* for all that occurs in our lives.

We accept You! Amen!

The Sabbath

"Remember the Sabbath day to keep it holy." (Exodus 20)
Jesus, help us to keep the Sabbath holy. The Sabbath is so sacred.
The Sabbath is a *gift* from God the Father to us all.
    Help us to worship, to pray, to praise You in a special way.
    Help us to rest from outward distractions,
    and feel Your presence in a beautiful way.
    The Sabbath is *God's* day—and *our* day.
    Help us to keep it so,
            to revere it again,
            to make it *special* again.
    May its holy peace pervade all of the earth,
            bestowing grace, mercy,
            refreshment, and love.
    May the Sabbath awaken the
            world—to Your love—Amen!

Loving

Jesus, You hung on the cross for us all.
Why did You do this, Lord?
Did You love us so much
      that nothing was too hard to do for us?
Help us to love in this way, also.
There is nothing too hard or impossible
      with love.
Jesus, give us this love! Amen.

Working

Jesus, You worked on earth
      the labor of Your hands—
          woodworking,
          carving,
          building,
          teaching—with love.
Jesus, help all of *our work* to be
      done in love.
                    Amen.

Healing

Jesus, stretch out Your hand
    and we *will* be healed!
                  Amen.

Coming

Jesus, there is no one—no one but *You*—
    who *can* help,
    who *can* come,
    who *can* save,
        us and all of humanity.
Jesus, come! Amen

All

Father, we release all into Your hands,
    all our lives,
        our fears,
    our illnesses,
    our sufferings,
    our trials.
Keep them *all* in Your heart.
We ask for help, for *all*,
            in Jesus's name.
              Amen.

Singing

Father, I sing to You when I am willing
    to set aside my doubts,
        and live free,
     free from any *mistrust*, free from
        any *fear*.
I sing when I am *happy*
    in *You*! Amen.

Singing makes me free to be myself by *enjoying* Your love. Help me *to* sing. Amen!

Truth

Father, say to our souls, "Have truth." Truth helps us to see *who* we really are—*Your children*! Amen.

Fear

Jesus, help us *not* to fear.
Fear drains us of our strength.
Give us our *strength*. Amen.

Loving, Caring, Sharing

Jesus, You were always there,
      loving, caring, sharing.
Help *us* to love, care, and
      share.

      Teach us how!

Jesus's Tears

Jesus, You cried on earth,
tears from God's Holy Son.
Wash the earth with those tears.
Wash us! Amen.

Walking

Jesus, we see You walking. Your footsteps are making patterns in the sand along the dusty roads—the footprints of God walking along the roads of earth.

Jesus, make all of our roads holy by Your footsteps.
Bless all of our journeys.

Amen.

Neglect

Dear Lord,
    Forgive us for the times
    that we didn't pray,
    that we didn't act,
    that we didn't do something
    that we *should* have done.
Jesus, forgive us!

Amen.

A Prayer for Those Contemplating Suicide

Jesus, I pray for those who are contemplating suicide. Help them to be stopped, dear Jesus, help them to see *You* and *who you* really are. *You are life!* Satan wants to *destroy* their lives. Help them to settle in *Your arms*. Help them to *choose* life. Help them to stay. Amen.

A Doctor's Prayer

Father, help me to be a good doctor. Help me to listen, to care, and to respect all in my care. Help me to give, to heal, to bless, using *Your* hands through mine. It is a privilege to become a doctor. May I use my knowledge in *Your* service. Amen.

A Prayer for Nurses

Father, help me to be a good *nurse*—kind, compassionate, caring, helpful, and loving. Help me to see *You* in *their* eyes.
Amen.

For Clergy

Jesus, bless all those entrusted to You in Your service, dedicated and consecrated to Your honor with their lives.

Help them to rely on *You.* They are to show *You* to the world. Help them to be a reflection of You, so that Your face will *shine in them.*

Show us You, in them. Amen.

For Students

Father, help me with my studies. I need Your help. Show me the way to truth, knowledge, wisdom, and respect.

There are many errors in life. Help me to discern and to grow in true knowledge that will benefit myself and others.

I offer my studying, my learning, to You.

Keep me safe.
Amen.

Love

Father, Your way is love. Teach us this love. Give us Your heart, and we will love. To love is to bring You honor. Make love our aim, to love without ceasing.

Show us this way to love in Jesus's name.
Amen.

Slavery

Jesus, the whole world is in slavery,
slavery to fear, to corruption,
greed, and the lust for power.
Jesus, save us by a word—
Let only Your word be said,
Your *will* be done,
and we will be free! Amen.

Lonely

Father,
When the way is lonely,
When I see no one,
Help me to see *You*!
Amen.

Little Children

"Let the little children come to Me,
    and forbid them not,
      for theirs is the Kingdom of Heaven."

(Matthew 19:14)

May *all* the children come to You,
    dear Jesus,
May all of *us* come to You—

Amen.

Respect

Father, teach us to respect all Your children. We are all Yours. We live, breathe, work, and play in Your heart. Never let us let You down, by any disrespect of others. When we look at others in any other way, it is sin. Help us *not* to sin. Instill in us *Your* respect for all. You love us as we are. You look away from our faults, our weaknesses, and see the good underneath. Help us to lift people up and not tear them down. Give us *Your* arms. Amen.

Treasuring

Jesus, what *do* we treasure in our lives?
Help us to treasure You!
You are *everything*
in all and through all.
Help us to see the treasure
in *You.*
Thank You, Jesus.
We love You, Jesus. Amen

Hurt

Father, I am hurting, sick, and confused. Bend my hurts into praise. Heal my sickness. Banish my confusion. Fill my hurts with peace, love, forgiveness, and kindness.

Father, help me to release the hurts and let love flow again. Help me to love.

I love You, Father. Amen.

Death

Lord, if we fear death,
Help us *not* to fear.
Help us to see death
    as *life*—
      a *new* life.
Give us *Your* life,
      dear Lord,
a life of love.
Help us to see that there
      is *no fear* in love,
and there is *no fear*,
      in death,
For death is only love,
      from You—
      Eternal life—
      Eternal love.
An eternity of love
      awaits us all.
Help us to see what
      Life really is—
      What *death* really is—
An awakening to a new life! Amen.

Release

There *is* a way to fight against all evil—
It is to pray—
Father, we *release all* into *Your hands,*
     We give *You* the task to *conquer* the evil.
     Do this *for* us, Father.
     We *praise* You for all!
Thank You, Father. Amen!

Bartimeus

Jesus, Bartimeus called out to You to receive His sight. (Mark 10:47)
Help *us* to call out to You
     to receive *our* sight,
     to see *all* that we must do,
     and to be *all* that we must be!

                           Amen.

"Jesus, Son of David,
     have mercy on me, a sinner."

                           Amen.

Youth

Jesus, help our youth.
We have tried in our society to make
     them "old" before their time.
We have allowed their time to be
     mismanaged,
by allowing them to be involved with
"entertainment" that robs them of
innocence, childhood, and happiness.
     Let everyone go back—
          to ideals—
          to family time—
          to caring—
          to sharing love at every turn.
Give all parents the blessedness of
     Your will for their lives and to share
this Gift with their children.
     Jesus, stretch out Your hand to
     bless the young. Amen.

Set Free

Father, we stand in front of You. You look at us. You see us, covered with sin, doubt, fear, and anguish.
But Father, *someone* is behind us.
Jesus is behind us.
He touches our shoulders.
We turn around to face Him.
We look into the eyes of Jesus.
He paid the price for us, Father, didn't He?

You look at us, now, Father,
Your eyes are searching our souls.
The blood of Jesus covers our souls,
   our bodies, our spirits.
We *are* set free—because of *Jesus.*

Father, look at us—
Now, *we are clean*—
      Amen!

Father

Dear Father in heaven,
    You have loved me when I was young,

    And you love me now.
    You love all people everywhere.

    Your heart is so big, it holds love for all.

    Father, I place *my* heart in
        Yours—so I can love all too!

Holy Spirit

Holy Spirit,
     Fill the earth with Your blessing.
Take charge of the earth.
Jesus said, "I will send you the Helper."
Help us now!
Take charge of the earth by
changing the earth.
Send the light to pierce the darkness.
Send the light to make all humanity free.
The light is real. We pray for the light.
We pray for *You* to come—

Come, Holy Spirit!
                Amen.

Teaching

Father, teach us to see all of Your blessings.
We have all that we need from You.
    Your hand holds all.
    We never have to fear.
Teach us never to be afraid.
You are with us in all of our dealings.
    You give us light and love.
    You show us joy.
You fill our souls with the breath of life.
You dispense Your blessings over all of the earth.
Teach us forgiveness, kindness, and love.
Never let us wallow in the darkness.
Help us to reach for the light and find it—in You! Amen.

Needs

Lord Jesus,
> When we are fearful,
> make us unafraid.

When we are lost,
> help us to find *You*.

When someone has hurt us,
> Let us give them Your forgiveness and ours!

When we are anxious,
Help us to see *You* with *us*.
You *are with us,* always!
Thank You, Jesus—for *You*! Amen.

Temptations

Jesus, help us with our temptations.
> Help us to say *no*.
> Help us to be strong in *Your* grace.
> Jesus, give us *Your* grace!
> > Amen.

Quiet

Father, we need to be quiet, we need to be still. Breathe upon us
Your stillness and peace. Help us to wait—to wait for the dawn—

The dawn *will come* if we wait.

Amen.

Reaping

Jesus, we reap what we sow.
(Galatians 6:7)
Help us to sow well. Help us to sow seeds of kindness, love,
encouragement, forgiveness, and peace in *our* part of the world.
Help us to be *great* sowers, and then we will be *great* reapers.

We will bring in the great harvest of love over all of the earth!

Amen.

Angels

Jesus, angels sang over Bethlehem, singing
  "Glory to God in the highest,
  and Peace on earth,
  good will to men" (Luke 2:14).

May angels sing *again* the same song, over
  all of the earth.
May *all* of humanity *hear* their singing.
May *all* of humanity—
  "Bend their swords into plowshares" and take heed of the words
of the angels:
May we all *look up* and *see* the angels in the sky and
  take their song to heart—

     "Glory to God in the
      highest
     and peace on Earth,
     good will to men."
        Amen!

A Meditation
Saving

Jesus, we see You as a tiny baby in Bethlehem. How beautiful You are! We see Your tiny hands and feet, Your eyes, so bright, showing the light of earth but also of heaven.

You see a star, shining in the night. What a beautiful star it is, but You *made* that star. You and the Father are *one, one* for all eternity. *All* creation is of Your making.

You lie in the manger, a feeding trough for animals. You see Mary, Your mother. She is beautiful, isn't she, Jesus?

There is a man there, a ruddy handsome man, a very hardworking man. He is Joseph, chosen to take care of You—teaching You and loving and caring for You as Your foster father.

You are a family, a holy family. We place *all* families in Your care. Bless them, help them, and save them, all over the earth.

Amen.

Later, Joseph teaches You how to plane wood. You will one day lie upon a wooden cross—to save a world—to save us all!

Thank You, Jesus, for coming to save us.

We love You, Jesus. Amen.

A Meditation
The Flight of Jesus into Egypt

Jesus, Joseph had to get up in the middle of the night and take Mary and You to Egypt. His heart must have been pounding as he heard the words from the angel.

"Get up! Hurry and take the Child and His mother to Egypt. Stay there until I tell you to return, because Herod is looking for the Child and wants to kill Him" (Matthew 2:13).

Joseph listened to the angel and got up and took Mary and You on the long journey to Egypt where You stayed until Herod died.

You were protected by Joseph and Mary. She cuddled You next to her heart and held You tightly as they made their way to Egypt.

The Father's love led You to Egypt.

Jesus, lead *us* to safety. Lead us on a safe road, on peaceful paths, near quiet streams.

"You lead me to streams of peaceful waters, and You refresh my life" (Psalm 23:2).

Jesus, lead *us* and keep us safe, always.

Amen.

A Secret

Jesus, the children You were with when You were growing up didn't know a secret. They were playing and with the Son of God! Did You have special friends calling out to You,
                "Jesus, come and play"?
Did You throw pebbles and play games with the children? Did You play with items Joseph had carved for You and Your friends from the carpenter shop?
They were unaware of the *magnitude* of the gift—God's own Son playing on the earth, as a little child.
Jesus, bless all the playing of the children all over the earth. Help the children *everywhere* to be *blessed* and *protected* by a special grace.
                Keep them safe, dear Jesus—
                                                Amen!

A Meditation on
"Come, Follow Me"

Jesus, You are looking at Andrew and Peter. *Come, follow* me, You think to yourself.

"Come, follow *me.*"

You tenderly approach Andrew. He is there by the boat—looking at You. What is in His eyes, dear Jesus? Does he realize that his life will never be the same?

You look at Him and think,

> *My apostle—my first. And then my second, not far behind.*

"Andrew, Peter, come follow *me* and I will make you fishers of men," is Your cry to them.

"Come, follow *me.*" They are about to embark on the greatest journey the world has ever known. There will be pain, hardship, suffering—untold suffering, suffering so great that even the skies would be darkened, for earth could not look at a Savior, a God, a man, suffering the crimes of an eternity—*our* eternity.

You look at them: Andrew with his piercing eyes. Not much is known about Andrew, but he is there, waiting to fulfill a destiny, to be a part of the twelve who *would* follow, who would partake in this greatest adventure—an adventure of love.

Are they ready? Peter looks at You. Poor, impetuous Peter—rough, headstrong, quizzical.

Who *is this man?* Peter thinks to himself, but then something happened, something that can never be explained except by *Your* magnitude—*Your* cry to them—and they come!

Immediately they leave their nets and follow You. Follow who? Follow a Savior though they knew it not then. Follow a man—but yet God—and this too, they didn't know.

But look, they *are* following, the two who would be joined by ten others.

The two brothers who were chosen in such a destiny to be partakers of dwelling with and sharing with You, this life of apostleship with their Savior.

Jesus, *You* look at *us.* There is the *same call* to us.

"*Come, follow me!*"

A Meditation on
The Woman at the Well

Jesus, You are talking to a woman at the well. "You are correct," You tell her, "You have no husband. The man that you are living with now, is *not* Your husband" (John 4:17–18).

She looks at You. "How do You know this? Are You a prophet, a *man* of God? Who *is* this man, she wonders, to know her soul, her very soul?

You tell her, "Everyone who drinks this water will get thirsty again. But no one who drinks the water *I* give will ever be thirsty again. The water I give will be like a flowing fountain that gives eternal life" (John 4:13–14).

She said, "Sir, give *me* this water, *that I may not thirst*" (John 4:15).

Jesus, give *us, too,* this *life-giving water.* You see all our sins, our doubts, and our fears, and yet You say to each one of us that You will give *us* the life-giving water *if* we ask. We do ask, dear Jesus.

The woman went to tell others that she had found the Messiah.

We too tell everyone that You are the Messiah, the king—of heaven and earth. Amen!

A Meditation
Jesus Is Nailed to the Cross

Jesus, the nails go deeply into Your sacred hands, and feet, and they anchor You to the cross. We stand by Your mother as she waits for them to lift You up on the cross.

Her head is bent in anguish. She is barely breathing. It is as if she *cannot* breathe, as if in breathing, it would make it even more real. She holds her breath—and then, she sees You there—hanging between heaven and earth.

She cannot look at Your pain, but she *can* look at Your eyes. You are her son and she loves You with an eternal love.

She gave You your earthly life, and now, You will give us all *new* life, by Your suffering and death.

Jesus, You are wounded for *us*—help *us* to offer *our* wounds in our lives for others, all *our* pain, grief, rejection, and heartaches.

We place *them* at the cross, *with You*. Make them jewels, dear Jesus—

Jewels for Your crown! Amen.

A Meditation
Jesus Dies on the Cross

We come to the cross, sweetest Jesus.
We see Your head bowed down,
We see tears in Your eyes,
    mingled with blood.
    Your body is writhing in pain.
    You try to raise Your head.
    You see the people there, the soldiers,
        the scribes, the pharisees, and
        You see Your loved ones.
        You look at them all,
        And You nod. "Yes, for *you*, for *you*, for
            you, for all," and . . .
   For us, also—Oh yes, for us!

"Lord Jesus, we are sorry for our sins. We do receive You as our Lord
and Savior of our lives—forever.
Take us and make us Yours—forever!"

                                        Amen.

A Meditation on
Jesus Is Taken Down from the Cross
and Laid in the Arms of His Mother

Jesus, it is finished. How glorious for You. Your eyes are closed, and You dwell in Your Father's realm.

The cross is empty, except for blood stains—*Your* blood, streaming down the wood.

Mary, You receive the body. What a blessing for you to hold in these few sacred moments, the body of a Savior. It is not only *your* Child that you hold now. You hold suffering and death conquered for all ages. The curtain in the temple is torn in two, the skies are darkened, the earth quakes. Jesus lies there in your arms, in your anguished arms.

But Mary, look at Him. *It is finished!* Satan is defeated by the body, the heart, the soul of Jesus. There is no more death. There is only *life*. The life—eternal life—will come to us all through this body that you hold. Praise God and alleluia! Satan's power will be no more!

A Meditation
The Appearance in the Upper Room

Jesus, You come into the upper room.
Suddenly You are there with Your
apostles.
They look at You—
You are their divine master.

Jesus, *we* look at You.
We see your nail-scarred hands.
We see your head—once crowned
with thorns—and your face—so
beautiful—so full of light.

Your body is radiant with light—
Your *robe* is shining like the *sun*.
You turn and look at *us*—
Jesus, *make us shine too*—
Help us *not* to be in the darkness—
through sin, doubt, fear, and remorse.
Let us live in Your kingdom of love
and light—forever! Amen.

Mercy

Mercy is God's rain
    falling
      on the earth.

Mercy is God's *love*—
making all things new.

Mercy is the heart of God
pouring out forgiveness,
    peace, wholeness,
        and healing.

Mercy is God—
    telling us—

I am healing—
I am forgiving—
I am opening
    my arms
to you—

      Forever!

Made in the USA
Coppell, TX
12 August 2023